CHRIST AND THE CHURCH

BEING THE THIRD PART OF A TREATISE ON

THE FORM OF THE SERVANT

BY THE SAME AUTHOR

A treatise on
The Form of the Servant

I
REVELATION AND
THE MODERN WORLD

II
THE DOMINION OF CHRIST

*

THE COMMON LIFE
IN THE BODY OF CHRIST
A Study of some of the Biblical Materials
for a Doctrine of the Church
Third edition

*

CONFIRMATION
Its place in the Baptismal Mystery

*

DACRE PRESS: A. AND C. BLACK

CHRIST AND THE CHURCH

*being the third part
of a treatise on*

THE FORM OF THE SERVANT

by

L. S. THORNTON, C.R.

D.D. CAMBRIDGE, HON. D.D. DURHAM

dacre press
westminster

FIRST PUBLISHED 1956

DACRE PRESS: A. AND C. BLACK LTD.
4, 5 AND 6 SOHO SQUARE, LONDON, W.1

PRINTED IN GREAT BRITAIN BY ROBERT MACLEHOSE AND CO. LTD
THE UNIVERSITY PRESS, GLASGOW

PREFACE

This volume completes the series entitled *The Form of the Servant* and includes the remaining material of my Scott Holland lectures. As in the two previous volumes the unity of revelation is the underlying theme; and the title indicates the particular sphere within which that unity is here considered. The subject is 'Christ and the Church' viewed as a single divine-human mystery; and once again it is assumed that this mystery which is both Christ and the church can be rightly understood only by paying careful attention to the forms and modes in which and through which it is unfolded in scripture. The argument presents a sequence of fundamental unities exhibited in the bible, some of which have already received attention in the preceding volumes. Where that is so, however, they are now presented in the particular forms which they assume in relation to the divinely given structure here contemplated. This applies, for example, to analogy and interrelation between the biblical accounts of creation and the new creation in Christ, or again to the story of our Lord's transfiguration in its bearing upon the life of the church. Attention is paid to the way in which the imagery of scripture sometimes transcends historical sequence, and again to an intensive organic unity between 'the last things' and the present form of the Christian life.

The original lectures have inevitably undergone some slight expansion; yet their lecture form has required very little alteration. Continuity of thought and considerations of space have compelled me to refer back not infrequently to detailed statements in my earlier published works. The concluding section of the last chapter contains material which first took shape in a sermon preached at All Saints' church, Margaret Street, on All Souls Day 1954. My thanks are due to all who have had a share in producing this book, and not least to Miss Margaret Webb for her accurate typing.

L. S. T.

June 1955

CONTENTS

Chapter II. THE CITY OF GOD

Chapter III. VOCATION AND WORSHIP

Chapter IV. CREATION AND WORSHIP

NOTE

ABBREVIATED references to my previous writings are, in the order of their publication, as follows:

The Common Life, Revelation, Dominion, Confirmation.

Other abbreviations are as in those works.

CHAPTER I

THE NEW CREATION MYSTERY

i

Two diverse lines of approach to scripture raise a problem of co-ordination. Fridrichsen on the unities of revelation. The function of tradition in scripture and the church. In a wide context revelation shows a three-fold pattern and a process of fulfilment.

In a recent volume issued by the Society for the study of the Old Testament[1] there were clearly perceptible two quite different lines of approach, each with its own characteristic technique. Of these the one represented the long-established methods of literary criticism whereas the other reflected predominantly 'anthropological' interests. The co-existence of two such markedly different lines of approach has already begun to raise important issues with regard to the nature of revelation, some of which have been discussed by me in previous volumes of this series. The way of approach which I have called anthropological has for some time been concentrating its attention upon the Old Testament, whereas, on the other hand, hitherto it has but slightly affected New Testament studies.[2] From the university of Uppsala, however, a principal centre of such interests, there has come appropriately a suggestion of possible developments extending also to this final deposit of revealed truth. I refer to an essay by Anton Fridrichsen, late Professor of New Testament exegesis.[3]

It should be clearer to us to-day than at any time in the past century that no single method of scientific study can effectually provide all the clues essential to our understanding of the biblical revelation. There is no question, therefore, of substituting one

[1] *The Old Testament and modern study* (Ed. H. H. Rowley, 1951, O.U.P.).

[2] But see the volume entitled: *The Primitive Christian Calendar* (C.U.P. 1952) by P. Carrington, Archbishop of Quebec.

[3] In a volume which he edited entitled *The Root of the Vine* (Dacre Press: A. & C. Black, 1953).

B   I

scientific technique for another, since all are equally necessary in so far as they are relevant. The real problem is one of co-ordination in a unified picture which does justice to all the facts. In the last resort this is fundamentally a theological problem which depends upon the nature of our connexion as Christians with that revelation which as believers we accept by faith. It is just here that the essay to which I have referred offers some illuminating suggestions. After reviewing critically the history of modern theories about the New Testament the author con-cludes with a series of statements about unity to which the previous argument has led, as follows: (1) 'The problem of Primi-tive Christianity is that of *the unity of the New Testament*'; (2) 'the problem of the unity of the New Testament is that of *the unity of the Church*'.[1]

The two statements just quoted are connected in the author's argument by a third, namely (3) 'the ground of unity is the Lord himself in unity with his Church'; and this, in turn, is understood to involve the conclusion (4) 'that in all the Scrip-tures the one Lord speaks through the one Church'.[2] Such an all-embracing conclusion certainly stands in need of elucidation. In the context of the argument it implies three things, first a close unity between the two Testaments; secondly the union of Christ and his Church in a single mystery; thirdly a close con-nexion between the unity of the Scriptures and ecclesiastical unity. In the author's mind the last-mentioned point has a mysterious nexus with the oneness of the Christ-mystery. For he says in close sequence two further things: (*a*) 'The New Testa-ment is an ecclesiastical book, and anyone using it to form and foster a private religion for himself abuses the Bible', and (*b*) 'only if Jesus is presented in unity with the Church . . . can the Gospel of the New Testament be seen and experienced as one and indivisible'(p. 60).

It is certainly true that our apprehension of unity in the New Testament is gravely impeded by the present divisions of Chris-tendom. For we approach the scriptures with very diverse presuppositions which have long since become traditional. More-over a purely literary analysis of biblical evidence is powerless to effect a transcendence over the theological limitations im-posed upon all of us by the tragedy of a shattered tradition.

[1] Italics as printed, *op. cit.*, pp. 61, 62.   [2] p. 61.

Actually the very function of church tradition as a medium through which revelation is received and interpreted has itself come to be viewed with suspicion, notwithstanding the inevitable dependence of each one of us upon that particular form of it in which we have been nourished. In such a situation it is possible that the anthropological approach might give us definite help by virtue of its large-scale familiarity with the workings of religious tradition. Something of this sort was indicated by Fridrichsen at a slightly earlier point in his essay. I refer to the paragraph beginning on page 55 in *The Root of the Vine*, in which the following sentences occur:

> The man of God is never isolated. He is always the centre of a circle taught by his words and example, in which his manner of life and teaching continues after his death. What is taught and written in this circle is ultimately derived from its founder, and embodies his life and character. When we, the children of a later age and of another culture, wish to underst̄ such a person and his period, we must return to tradition and inquire there; but our inquiry must be made with due understanding of local peculiarities. Only with such a sympathetic understanding is it possible to estimate a tradition as a source of history.

He goes on to say that in the situation envisaged 'tradition is an excellent source for history'. For 'no biographical or psychological account of such figures can be given. . . . Real understanding is only possible after considering the legacy they leave to their circles, and the tradition formed, preserved and continually propagated within them'.

What has just been quoted concerning the function of tradition as the nexus of a religious group having its centre and focus in a leader touches one aspect only of a sociological process which must now be presupposed as a background to the bible as a whole. Tradition here takes on a much wider and more many-sided form, providing for the people of God a solid continuity, religious and cultural, stretching through the centuries of biblical history. From this point of view it would seem that the anthropological approach is inevitably presenting a challenge to a certain one-sidedness which characterizes the technique of current literary analysis. Not only in Germany, but also nearer home, it seems to be largely taken for granted that adequate clues to the meaning of New Testament writings can be found primarily in the phraseology of other religious litera-

3

ture of approximately the same period. Parallels there certainly are; but a parallel is not necessarily a source; and the assumption that it always is ignores the whole character of a *Weltanschauung* in which a common level of mental development is reflected on a broad front in the interplay of diverse cultural traditions from a correspondingly complex background.

The immediate and fundamental background to the New Testament is, of course, set before us in the Old Testament, to which later Judaism also provides an important appendage. The religion of Israel, however, unique as it is in its character as the channel of a special revelation, should not be regarded simply as an isolated phenomenon, but rather as the divinely chosen *locus* of a widely extended interplay between religious and cultural forces, forces which spread out far beyond the limits of Israel's national life. This extended interplay continued to operate in the Christian era, providing for the New Testament its wide contemporary context. In that context of contemporary religious culture points of contact are rightly sought and found. The search, however, may easily prove to be unprofitable or even misleading unless equal attention is given to other factors of primary importance. Of these one has been emphasized in the above quotation from Fridrichsen concerning the nexus between a religious leader and his circle of disciples; another primary factor is the corresponding nexus with the historical tradition of a far-stretching yet continuous past.

In the present volume these two modes of continuity are to be considered in their mutual relations. The unity between Christ and the Church in a single divine-human mystery is to be set upon the background of Israelite tradition which binds the two Testaments together in a corresponding unity. Both of these are essentially scriptural unities and therefore also dominant strands in the pattern of revelation. But if we are to apprehend rightly 'the very varied wisdom of God'[1] manifested in that revelation we must take full account of a third strand in the pattern, namely the close interweaving of redemptive history with the theme of creation for which, in the preceding volume of this Series I coined the phrase: 'A Genesis-Exodus mystery.'[2] Lastly this conception of a threefold pattern needs to be supplemented by the apostolic doctrine of a fulfilment, perfecting or recapitu-

[1] Eph. 3¹⁰.   [2] *Dominion*, pp. 48 *f.*

4

lation in Christ. The plan of creation is not only restored in
Christ. Until the Incarnation that plan was not fully disclosed.
From this point of view the two biblical mysteries, Christ and
creation, are mutually complementary. Neither can be rightly
apprehended apart from the other.

ii

The comparison of death and resurrection with sowing and
reaping (John 12²⁴) suggests a contrast between the realism of
Christ's sacrifice and all 'escapist' cults, ancient or modern. The
integral relation between the death and the resurrection of Jesus.
In biblical idiom Christ the firstfruits is both 'head' and 'sum-
total'. His body is the place of sacrifice in which creaturely sonship comes to fruition.

In our approach to the new-creation mystery let us start from
some dominical sayings about sowing and reaping reported by
St John (4³⁵⁻³⁸) immediately after the sacrificial saying of 4³⁴.
The sower prepares the harvest for the reapers to gather. So the
sacrifice of Christ was the seed-sowing from which we gather
fruits into life eternal (cp. 12²⁴). Now the myths of dying and
rising gods were also connected with that cycle of death and re-
birth which is a universal characteristic of nature. In the later
forms assumed by those ancient religious cults, however, there
was something strangely paradoxical. For, having originally
identified the divine with nature, they now sought to provide
for their adherents, by means of this very identification, a way
of escape from nature. The cult of the mystery-god thus became
a way of escape from the world, whereby, however unwittingly,
men blasphemed the Creator in his creatures. For, in effect, they
first worshipped nature and then deserted it. This combination
of idolatry and escapism is the fruit of man's primal disobedience. When we grasp at the fruits of nature lawlessly for our
own ends, those fruits turn sour to the taste; so in the end we
cast them aside in disgust and disillusionment. If they are to be
truly enjoyed, the resources of nature must be offered to the only
true God.

Such an offering, however, involves 'sacrifice' in the full depth of
its meaning. In its modern connotation the word often suggests

no more than the foregoing of lesser satisfactions in order that a major advantage may be gained. In its true meaning, however, sacrifice is not worldly wisdom but worship. It is a filial response to our heavenly Father whereby we recognize and acknowledge his goodness as the source of all his creaturely gifts. Thus through communion with him, and only so, we enjoy the fruits of his fatherly bounty. To this relationship sin is the obstacle; and for sin the sacrifice of Christ was the indispensable act of redress by which man's true relationship to God was restored, and thus the gates of the earthly paradise were re-opened. In this sense it would be true to say that Christianity is the only genuine mystery religion. For it is the only religion of a dying and rising God which does not eventually seek for escape from nature. It involves, not an abandonment of this earthly creation, but its restoration to its true use through re-creation.

Instead of usurpation it shows the way of sacrifice and that transfiguration of life which comes through sacrifice in the full depth of its meaning. Instead of disillusionment and escape from earthly ills it offers a realistic facing of all ills in the way of the cross which is also the way of resurrection. For as the seed only bears fruit through dying and rising, so the rich fruits of human life can be gathered only through a dying and rising with Christ. The dying, however, is integral to the rising. This is indicated in the wounds which the risen Lord showed in his glorified body. It is this aspect of the resurrection which sets it in contrast to all merely utopian dreams of earthly happiness. For in all such dreams the transition from the actual to the ideal is fortuitous. There is no essential connexion between present experience and that which the heart desires. An artificial connexion has to be made through the popular myths of evolution and progress. This is really no better than a technique of escape disguised under high-sounding words.

The scars upon the body of the risen Lord reveal the positive significance of sacrifice as truly as the harvest shows the justification of the seed-sowing. Resurrection is not escape from a dying life. It *is* the dying life brought to fruition. For death is not the end of sacrifice, but the mode of operation through which sacrifice takes effect. Death is not an end but the means to that fulness of sacrificial life which is the only complete life. This makes clear the integral connexion between the death and the resurrection of Jesus. He was glorified *in* the death and *through* the resurrection. In the death the sacrifice was completed; through the resurrection the fruition of the completed sacrifice was secured. The mortal flesh was the sanctuary in which the sacrifice was effected; the risen body is that same sanctuary transformed into the permanent temple of humanity, at the heart of which is the eternal treasure of the finished sacrifice.[1] Once more, the scars in the risen body which indicate the sacrifice also signify the conquest of the hostile powers by the sacrificial victim. Lastly, this temple of the body which is both the place of sacrifice and the scene of messianic triumph is also the permanent abode of that Spirit with which the New Man was anointed for sacrifice and equipped for victory.[2]

The new creation began when 'the last Adam' who is 'from heaven' was 'conceived by the Holy Ghost' and so became, as man, 'a life-giving spirit.'[3] That was like the seed-time of the new harvest,[4] whereas the firstfruits were gathered in when Christ rose from the dead.[5] Then, however, the Son of David dispossessed his enemies and claimed his inheritance; then he received the messianic dominion. Only then was he able to exercise in their fulness the functions of 'the last Adam', which were his from the first.[6] As the Word incarnate he unites in himself the divine attributes of the Creator-Word and the cosmic functions of the divine-human Head of creation. In his risen glory, therefore, he is able to re-create our fallen nature, breathing into it once more the divine Spirit of whose fulness he himself partakes in his anointed humanity.[2] The New Man, as the firstfruits of the new creation, embodies the promise of the whole harvest. For in him creation has already come to fruition. No single image, however, can do justice to the facts. For example, as firstfruits he identifies himself by anticipation with

---

[1] cp. *Dominion*, pp. 131–137 and *The Apostolic Ministry*, pp. 86–93, 99–104.

[2] Fuller details in my book on *Confirmation* (A. & C. Black, 1954), pp. 96–132.

[3] 1 Cor. 15[45, 47], Luke 1[35]; cp. St John's use of the expressions: 'from above' and 'from heaven'.

[4] It would seem that in the thought of St John the seed 'fell into the earth' (12[24]) when the Word who is the Seed of the Father was sown in the Virgin's womb, cp. *Dominion*, pp. 123–126.

[5] 1 Cor. 15[20, 23].

[6] 1 Cor. 15[24–28], Rom. 1[3, 4], Col. 1[18], Heb. 2[5–10].

the harvest which is to come, whereas, on the other hand, in his risen and ascended glory he is also the heavenly reaper of whom we read in the Revelation of St John (14[14-16]).

It is, however, a fact that in the biblical languages the words for 'firstfruits' are etymologically connected with ideas of headship and rule.[1] Moreover, as Adam included his descendants, so 'beginning' or 'first' may carry a nuance of inclusiveness, and thus come to mean 'sum-total'. A verbal interplay of this kind is manifest in Colossians 1[12-20]. Thus the messianic 'head' of the church is also the 'body', and the firstfruits will eventually be found to include the whole harvest. As the Son of Man enthroned upon the cloud and crowned with the victor's wreath of gold Jesus holds in his hand the sharp sickle of the final harvesting. He is the arbiter of human destiny, because through and in him alone can mankind attain to its goal. So, too, he is the conqueror whose hands take and open the sealed book of destiny,[2] inasmuch as the all-prevailing sacrifice of the preordained victim is the master-key to the course of human history. Redemption, however, is effected not only 'through him' but also 'in him'. For by sharing our nature he 'tabernacled in us', in order that in the sanctuary of his body redeemed humanity might be taken up into his self-offering. Thus it will be that at the final ingathering the firstfruits will include the harvest.

In that new order of life which Jesus inaugurated his mortal flesh was, once for all, the place of illumination, conflict and judgement. So, too, in that same order 'the temple of his body' is 'the place' of transfiguration, worship and fruition. The conflict in the flesh was won through the perfecting of obedience; and the sacrifice thus offered was taken up into the transfigured life of the risen body. There it is the foundation of that worshipful life in which alone created sonship can come to fruition. For the finished sacrifice of the risen Lord is the very substance of that embodied response to the Father in which the whole creation was designed to attain its consummation.[3]

[1] In Hebrew *reshîth* with *r'ôsh*, and in Greek *aparché* with *arché*.

[2] Rev. 5[1-7].

[3] The phraseology of this paragraph can be illustrated from *Dominion*, Chs. 4–6. Also for 'the temple of his body' see *Apostolic Ministry*, p. 104; and for 'the place', *Revelation*, p. 176 and p. 221, note 2.

iii

The Church integral to the 'new creation' mystery of the Christ. The analogy with the first creation suggests a close relation between the New Eve and the dominion of the Christ. A Christian re-interpretation of the creation narratives finds a single plan of the Creator, foreshadowed in Genesis, but fully disclosed only in the incarnate Lord. The threefold headship in 1 Corinthians 11[3].

Rooted and grounded in the great act of restoration which Christ has effected, and inseparably associated with all the consequences of that act in history, stands the redeemed community, the Church of the new creation, not simply a historical institution but also a mystical entity, the significance of which can be rightly understood only by reference to the total 'mystery of the Christ'[1] to which it belongs. Two consequences follow from this line of approach. First, the doctrine of the church is no mere appendix or corollary of the Christian faith. It belongs to its substance. Everything which concerns the church is integral to the central dogmas of Christian theology. Secondly, if the church is bound up in this way with the Christian revelation as a whole, then it must have a vital connexion with the Christian doctrines concerning creation and man. For our present purpose this will mean that the new creation embraces in one single mystery both the existence of the church and the dominion of Adam restored in Christ. As unfolded in scripture the doctrine of the church is not only the doctrine of a new Israel. It also rests upon an analogy between the two creations.

In developing its thesis concerning the mystery of the Christ the Epistle to the Ephesians draws a detailed picture of the mystical union between Christ and the church (5^{22-33}). In this picture it is clear that Christ is regarded as the new Adam; and by consequence the church fulfils the rôle of a new Eve. In accordance with various statements in the earlier Pauline epistles the conception of the church as the bride of Christ is here related to the analogy elsewhere drawn between the two creations.[2] Two points in the analogy are of immediate importance, both of them being connected with the Christian interpretation of the creation narratives in Genesis 1 and 2. The

---

[1] Eph. 3[4].   [2] e.g. 1 Cor. 11[3 *ff*], 2 Cor. 11[2 *ff*], Rom. 5[12 *ff*].

9

points referred to concern (1) the explanations given in those narratives with regard to the union of man and woman and (2) the close connexion in which those explanations stand to what is said about the dominion of Adam. In considering these details we have to remember that for the New Testament authors Genesis 1 and 2 would together yield a single picture. The two narratives would be regarded as complementary sources of information about one set of events. Here, as elsewhere, the Christian theologian must read Genesis through the eyes of the first Christians.

(1) In Genesis 1 [27] we read that 'God created the man[1] in his own image, in the image of God created he him, male and female created he them'. If this statement is understood in the light of the story in Genesis 2 concerning the origin of Eve we get a single picture. First the man alone was created (2 [7]), and then the woman was 'taken out of man' (2 [23]). The two statements together indicate first the creation of a single organism ('the man'), and then the division of this single organism into two individuals, the man and the woman. Thus there were two creative acts of God. First he created the new species—'man' or 'Adam'[2]—in the male form, and imparted to it his image. Then by a further creative act he formed the two out of the one, differentiating the woman from the man in whom she had previously been included. But further, the two, although now differentiated, are still 'one flesh' (2 [24]). For in the Hebrew way of thinking a man includes within himself the human beings who are his physical issue. These conceptions would lie behind the twofold doctrine of the church as both the Body and the Bride of Christ.

(2) The second point to be noticed is that in both of these narratives the dominion over the lower creation, granted to man, is closely related to the other details which have just been given. In the first chapter of Genesis the grant of the dominion is twice mentioned immediately after reference has been made to the creation of man. In the second reference it would be natural to infer that the dominion is granted jointly to both sexes (1 [27, 28]). In the second chapter the dominion is represented in two ways, first by the statement that Adam is put in

---

[1] *Lit:* 'the Adam'; see below.
[2] The Hebrew phrase ('the Adam') could mean 'humanity' or 'the human race'.

charge of the garden, and secondly by the fact that Adam gives names to the animals. Both of these events occur before the creation of Eve. But the latter incident is expressly connected with Adam's need of a companion and helper in his solitary eminence over the other creatures. Once more a single picture results, in which the man has the priority. The dominion is granted explicitly to him; but after the creation of the woman she shares his responsibilities as his indispensable partner. This sharing of responsibility becomes evident in the ensuing story of Eve's temptation. Finally the 'rule' of man over woman is represented as a consequence of the fall. The companionship of Paradise is replaced by a less ideal relationship.[1] In compensation, however, Eve is still 'the mother of all living' (3^{20})—an expression which seems to set her, with Adam, over all creation.

Accordingly, when St Paul says that 'the man is head of the woman' he might be supposed to be drawing a deduction from the narrative of Genesis. For him, however, this statement depends upon another: 'I would have you know that the head of every man is the Christ.'[2] In fact he is arguing, not from creation to Christ, but from Christ to creation. His convictions concerning the matter in question rest, not upon the authority of 'Moses', but upon 'the mystery of the Christ'. He found in the story of Adam a foreshadowing of Christ's headship over creation. Adam was 'head' in order that he might foreshadow the headship of Jesus. In other words the first creation was part of a much larger plan which was from the first Christo-centric. In fact the details of the first creation were determined by the predestined order of the second. From 1 Corinthians 11^3 we may now draw two further conclusions. First, it is clear that for the apostle a single plan or pattern runs through divine revelation. For Christ is not simply a second Adam brought in to undo the first man's disobedience. He has all along, from the beginning, been the true head of creation. In short the thesis unfolded in Ephesians 5 is already implicit in the earlier epistle. A connecting link between the two may be found in the intermediate statement of 2 Corinthians 4^{4-6}.

Christ alone is, in the fullest sense, the image and glory of God. So, until the Incarnation the plan of creation was not fully

---

[1] Gen. 3^{16} ; contrast 2^{23}, to which Hos. 2^{18} may refer.
[2] 1 Cor. 11^3.

revealed. It was still a *mysterion*, that is a divine secret awaiting disclosure in the fulness of time according to God's will. It is from this point of view that the two biblical mysteries, Christ and creation must be judged to be mutually complementary, so that neither can be rightly apprehended apart from the other.[1] Returning then to our interpretation of I Corinthians 11[3] we may conclude that its second statement—'the man is the head of the woman'—is not simply a deduction from Genesis; for it implies a Christian re-interpretation of the order found in Genesis. Its meaning will be drawn from the headship of the Christ. Secondly, the Christian meaning of headship is indicated in the final clause of St Paul's statement: 'God is head of the Christ.' The second Adam, like the first, is God's viceroy; his headship is the counterpart of obedience. The headship of the Christ was manifested in lowly submission to the will of his Father. It is not the 'rule' of fallen Adam, but the pre-eminence of God's true Servant.[2]

iv

The form of creation determined by its end in Christ. By his death he took possession of the restored dominion and became Bridegroom of the new Israel. The connexion of the church with the restored dominion depends upon the two meanings of 'one flesh' (body and bride), which, in St John, correspond to two stages of the new creation: (1) the incarnate Word; (2) 'the Spirit and the Bride'. In our present union with Christ there is both identity and contrast, with continuity of mission.

The preceding analysis suggests that for apostolic thought the typical images of the Old Testament *presuppose* their fulfilment in the total mystery of the Christ. This will mean, for example, that, whereas the first creation foreshadows the second creation, it does so precisely because its own form is determined by the necessity that it shall find its fulfilment in the Christ. This agrees with what was said in the preceding volume concerning the doctrine that all things are to be summed up in the Christ,

[1] cp. above, the concluding sentence of § i.

[2] cp. Mark 10[42-45] and John 13[13-15], 15[15] with par. 4 of this section (conclusion and note).

as stated in Ephesians 1 [10].[1] The significance of this world-order can be disclosed only in Jesus, because he is the mould in which it was made as well as the end towards which it moves. This principle is further illustrated in that section of Ephesians which interprets the relations between Christ and the Church. 'A man is head of his wife as also the Christ is head of the church' (5 [23]). Here the earthly relationship is to conform to a heavenly pattern to which it has always pointed. This conformation of human society to the heavenly pattern will later receive further consideration. At present, however, we will continue to trace the heavenly pattern by means of the analogy between the two creations, the first of which foreshadows the second.

In that analogy it is important that we should distinguish between headship and dominion. 'Adam was first formed, then Eve.'[2] Headship is the privilege of God's firstborn Son; and in this Adam prefigures our Lord's title as 'the beginning of the creation of God'.[3] The dominion is, however, associated with the creation of the woman. Jesus is 'the man from heaven', the new head of creation, who in his own right is 'the head of every man'. To him, therefore, 'all things were delivered' by the Father in order that he might recover possession of his inheritance. This inheritance was none other than the dominion of Adam, usurped by fallen man in the interest of the hostile powers. In his conquest of those powers Jesus took possession, not only of the stronghold of Zion, but also of the whole universe. Moreover, this he did by that same act by which, in the death of the cross, he took to himself as his bride the redeemed people of God. So there is a close connexion between the creation of the new Eve and the restoration of Adam's dominion, as in the original story there was a close connexion between the bestowal of the dominion and the creation of a helpmeet as the consort of creation's head.

Thus the church is the partner of the Christ in the messianic kingdom which he has won. She was created to share with him the joys of the new creation in paradise regained. Of this 'sharing', however, two aspects are prefigured in Genesis, corresponding to the two distinct meanings there given to the expression: 'one flesh.' The phrase indicates, on the one hand, the sharing of a common nature in organic identity and, on the

---

[1] *Dominion*, pp. 4–6.   [2] 1 Tim. 2 [13].   [3] Rev. 3 [14].

other hand, the intimate union of two persons in one life on the basis of the common nature shared. In the nuptial section of Ephesians (5^{22-33}) these two conceptions are blended by a play on the double meaning of the keywords: 'head', 'body' and 'flesh'. Accordingly, we may think in terms of a single organism in which Christ is the head and the church is the body. It will then follow that everything which happened to our Lord from the moment when he became incarnate has also happened to the church in him. But we may also think of the 'one flesh' as a mystical union of the New Man with his bride, regarding the unity in terms, not of simple identity, but of personal intimacy and mutual responses. Both images are necessary to a right understanding of the connexion between the church and the restoration of Adam's dominion.

In one passage where the context suggests the bridal relationship St Paul refers to individual union with our Lord in terms of 'one spirit'. Here the mystical union is deliberately contrasted with the 'one flesh' of a casual sex-union; and there follows a reference to the indwelling of the Holy Spirit.[1] Similarly 'the Spirit and the Bride' are explicitly associated in the Apocalypse.[2] But the subject is most fully developed in St John's Gospel; there two stages are indicated in the union of Christ with his people. For first he became one flesh with us through his Incarnation; and, secondly, by his death, resurrection and ascension he handed over to us his Spirit. In his earthly life his flesh was already the place of mystical abiding (15^{1-11}); yet his departure was expedient, that by the coming of the Spirit the bride might attain the identity of a fully distinct existence as complement of the Bridegroom. Thus St John brings to its most complete development the analogy with the story of Eve's creation. In so doing he includes the distinctive existence of the church within that cluster of mysteries which he has so wonderfully integrated into the one all-embracing mystery of the new creation.[3]

This integration of all mysteries into one corresponds symbolically to the Synoptic handling of our Lord's Transfigura-

[1] I Cor. 6^{15-20}.
[2] Rev. 22^{17}.
[3] For details see *The Apostolic Ministry*, pp. 98–101 and *Confirmation*, pp. 177 *ff*.

tion.[1] Its Johannine treatment, however, has the effect of exhibiting a complete identity of existence as between Christ and the church, notwithstanding the differentiation between his present mode of existence and ours which was finally effected through death and resurrection. As his flesh was not left behind, but taken up into a life wholly quickened by the Spirit, so the principle of the 'one flesh' continues to hold good in our union with him' through partaking of his Spirit. As the scars of his mortal flesh appeared in the risen body, so the sacrificial life offered in that flesh is manifested in the lively members of that same body. Thus there is a reproduction in the church of the law and pattern exhibited successively in his earthly life and passion, in his death and resurrection, in his risen and ascended life. The doctrine of the 'one flesh', by which Christ and the church for ever share one life, has therefore a second application through the bestowal of the Spirit, the two modes of identification corresponding to the two stages in the creation story. The two applications of the law may now be stated together:

(i) All that happened to the incarnate Lord happened to the church in him;
(ii) All that so happened to him and in him now happens in the church by mystical union with him.

Thus, when Jesus died, rose and ascended into heaven the Israel of God died upon the cross, rose from the tomb and ascended to be where he is. Yet all this, which happened once for all in the historical past of Jesus and his church, happens now continuously in this present dispensation in accordance with a perennially renewed pattern. This doctrine of identity, however, must be balanced by a necessary distinction. The identity between Christ and the church cannot be affirmed too strongly provided that we recognize the differentiation between his mode of existence and ours, the contrast (that is) between his session in heavenly glory and our present earthly pilgrimage. The two sides of the truth are tersely summed up in the Johannine saying: 'As he is, even so are we in this world.' Our life is one with his; yet ours is lived 'in the world', as his once was, but

[1] For which see *Dominion*, Ch. 6.

(in that sense) is no longer.[1] When Jesus was 'in this world' the wealth of the 'all things' delivered to him was exhibited in the outward form of poverty. His headship was exercised in obedience to his Father by fulfilling the lowly destiny of the Servant. So it is with the church. As the consort of Christ the head, she already shares with him the resources of his messianic dominion. By partaking of his Spirit, however, she is enabled to partake in his obedience. The wealth of the Spirit's endowment which she receives from her victorious Lord equips her to fulfil in the world that sacrificial vocation which he fulfilled in his earthly course. His conflict is continued in the church until all his enemies are put under his feet.

V

As in the human body one life is present simultaneously in all events, so, in the mystery of Christ and the church the Whole transcends its historical sequence, so that every event in the new creation has the significance of the whole. Yet also the sequence is cumulative; e.g. the sacrifice is taken up into glory, and the obedience perfected in death inaugurates (a) the new name of Jesus as Lord, imprinted upon his members, and (b) the bridal co-operation of the church as firstfruits of redeemed humanity.

This doctrine of identity in distinction must now be related to the conception of the new creation as embracing in a single mystery both the being of the church and the restored dominion of Adam. From one point of view the church is included in the one divine-human organism which is the Christ. The 'one flesh' is then understood on the analogy of one individual life. In such a single life head and body, or whole and parts, are one—and that not simply in continuity of existence, or in identity of form, or even in uniformity of pattern. They are also one in the sense that the life common to head and body, or whole and parts, is shared, not successively, but *simultaneously* throughout the organism. The succession of events within the whole falls within this simultaneity of life in the whole. Thus, in our bodies the circulation of the blood takes place through a succession of events.

---

[1] I John 4[17]; cp. John 17[11]. For another sense in which he enters the world again, see below, Ch. II, § ii, last par., etc.

Yet the one life of the body is present in, or characterizes, all such events, being present throughout the whole to which they belong. Similarly anything which happens to the head happens also to the whole body and affects every member of it. The event is simultaneous to the whole and its parts, because the life which that event affects is one and simultaneous.[1]

So what happened to Christ happened to us. We died, when he died upon the cross.[2] We rose with him. Because he ascended we are 'seated with him in the heavenly places'.[3] Thus, as sharer in the messianic kingdom the church is already co-partner with her Lord in that dominion of Adam which he has restored. It will be remembered, however, that Adam's dominion is wholly conditioned by obedience to the divine will. So also the restored dominion is the fruit of Christ's obedience in his redemptive activity, being inseparable from it. In fact the restoration pre-supposes his humiliation. Moreover, as the risen body includes the marks of the nails, so the messianic glory includes the finished sacrifice. The exaltation, therefore, not only presup-poses, but actually includes within itself the whole pattern of the 'self-emptying', that is, the sacrificial libation which flowed from heaven to earth when the Word became flesh, that out-pouring of life which was finally consummated in the death on the cross.[4] At this point, then, we may recall what was said earlier concerning the truth that death and resurrection to-gether form one mystery of the new creation.[5] Moreover, in the previous volume it was suggested that in the gospels this prin-ciple of interpretation is extended backwards and forwards until the whole gospel story and the life of the church are together subsumed under that one mystery.[6]

[1] Parts developed later (such as new skin) may bear marks (e.g. of a scar) which were incurred long before those particular parts existed. More-over in the analogy it must be remembered that for biblical thought all sub-sequent members or generations of the 'body politic' are present in the head as founder. Cp. Heb. 7[9, 10].

[2] This is expressly affirmed by St Paul in 2 Cor. 5[14].

[3] The threefold use of the preposition 'with' in Eph. 2[5, 6] has the effect of making our transformation simultaneous 'with' the glorification of the Christ.

[4] St Paul's application of the 'libation' image to himself in Phil. 2[17] sug-gests that he had the same imagery in mind in his account of our Lord's *kenosis* in 2[7].

[5] See above, § ii.   [6] See especially, *Dominion*, Ch. VI.

The end, therefore, is implicit in the beginning as surely as the beginning is like a seed which contains within itself all its future development. So the whole wealth of the Godhead was present in the self-impoverishment of the Christ, as this in turn included within itself his glorification and our enrichment.[1] All the effects of grace in the church were implicit in what Jesus was at each stage of the gospel story; and so also the whole pattern of his sacrifice and of its fruits is present now in the redeemed community. Thus the order and character of the new creation has a unity which transcends the actual unfolding of the history. This, however, does not depreciate the history; on the contrary, every event of that history has surpassing importance, because it is charged with that significance which belongs to the whole mystery of the Christ. The fulness of the mystery both includes, and is included in, all its events. In this sense the church was always included in the Christ. In this sense the New Eve was created in the New Man; and (as St John affirms) our new beginning was wrapped up in his divinely-wrought human beginning.[2]

So far, in this section, we have been interpreting identity in terms of the one body, 'one flesh' being understood to mean one organism. In the apostolic writings, however, this imagery always implies mutual co-operation, as between whole and parts or head and members, and again between one member and the others. The social conception is never absent from the idea presented. It easily passes, therefore, into the alternative picture of husband and wife. Here, then, the 'one flesh' of Eve's origin in Adam has, in the analogy, acquired two additional aspects, namely (1) a mystical union of two persons and (2) their mutual co-operation on the basis of that union and its shared life. Such co-operation, again, means partnership in fulfilment of a common purpose. This, however, is precisely what is signified by the dominion of Adam. Man has been made a partner of the Creator in the carrying out of the latter's plan for the world. The response of creation to its Creator is to be mediated through the obedience of its human head. This parallel between two forms of co-operation is a further link between the two concepts of the New Eve and the restored dominion.[3]

[1] cp. 2 Cor. 8⁹. [2] John 1¹²⁻¹⁴. cp. *Dominion*, pp. 114–121.
[3] It suggests also that the statement of threefold headship in 1 Cor. 11³ has a Christo-centric reference throughout. See above, end of § iii.

The response of creation to its Creator through human media-
tion was present in its fulness in the Christ. For he had placed
himself within the creation precisely in order that through his
obedience its whole movement might be redirected towards
God. The response was, therefore, implicit (if only in germinal
form) in all those who, by accepting the Christ, came to 'believe
on his name'. Only, however, when his obedience was completed on the cross in death could their response become fully
operative. The fruits of his finished sacrifice could now be manifested in the new Israel which he had formed. Thus the bride
attained to a fully distinct existence through the death of the
bridegroom. Once more the type was fulfilled in its antitype.
The new Eve was formed out of the new Adam at precisely that
moment when he fell asleep upon the cross on the sixth day of
the new creation. Moreover, there was one further consequence
of the perfected response. For his 'obedience unto death' the
second Adam received on our behalf that name which is his by
right, 'the name which is above every name.' The elect Servant
was then acknowledged by the Father as Lord of all. In his
humiliation he was known as 'Jesus'. But when he had restored
the lost dominion he was recognized as *kyrios*, that is 'Lord' of
heaven and earth, the true head of creation.[1]

Adam gave 'names' to all the creatures. Jesus imprinted his
own 'new name' upon all who became new creatures in him.[2]
Man is able to recognize and appraise the diverse characteristics which distinguish the works of God, and thus to relate
them to himself. This truth is symbolized in the naming of the
animals by Adam. But the superiority thus implied can be
rightly exercised only by one who co-operates in the Creator's

---

[1] In Phil. 2⁹⁻¹¹, 'the name' is represented by the primitive Christian confession of faith: κύριος Ἰησοῦς Χριστός (Jesus Christ is Lord). The background
here is Isa. 45 ¹⁸⁻²⁵ (LXX), where, in vv. 18, 19, the divine name (JHVH)
is represented by ἐγώ εἰμι Κύριος. This phrase covers two of the divine
titles, as revealed to Moses in Exod. 3¹⁴, ¹⁵, a passage which also concludes
with the statement: 'this is my name.' Moreover, the prophecy in Isa. 45²³:
'every knee shall bow to me' (i.e. to God) is, according to Phil. 2¹⁰, fulfilled
when every knee bows 'at the name of Jesus'. The name given in Phil. 2⁹ is,
therefore, κύριος as applied to Jesus. This fulfilment is represented in
dramatic form in John 18¹⁻¹¹, on which see *The Apostolic Ministry*, p. 97,
note 2.

[2] Rev. 3¹², 14¹; cp. also 2 Cor. 5¹⁷, John 10³, Rev. 2¹⁷; and see further
below, Ch. III, for fuller development of this theme.

plan. This destiny was fulfilled by Jesus who is the true head of every man. He alone imparts his own new name; for he imparts his own lowly character and sovereign characteristics to all his subjects in the new creation. In acknowledging his headship they become partakers in his obedience and already enjoy its fruits in the earthly paradise to which it gives entrance. They 'reign' with him 'upon the earth' as they are enthroned with him in heaven.[1] He alone is 'Lord'; but in his lordship the reign of obedient man is restored. In those who acknowledge his headship, therefore, he receives a helpmeet, a bride who is herself the firstfruits within his dominion. For we are 'a kind of firstfruits of his creatures'.[2] This conception of the church as 'firstfruits' of creation gives her a mediatorial function in relation both to God and to man. At the same time it defines her position as the meeting-place of two worlds, marking out its limits in both directions.

The biblical use of this term (firstfruits) is threefold. The church has inherited Israel's position as the firstfruits of mankind.[3] She is dedicated to God in no exclusive sense, but simply as the first instalment of an offering whose fulness will be the whole of redeemed humanity. But secondly, we have this privilege solely as partakers in Christ. For he alone, as the new Adam, is the firstfruits in his own right by virtue of his sinless self-oblation to the Father.[4] He is the firstfruits of the new creation; and we, in him, are the firstfruits of the world which he has redeemed. Moreover, thirdly, we have this privilege because we have received the firstfruits or first instalment of the Spirit,[5] with whose fulness Jesus was anointed, whose plenitude he ever enjoys. Thus, the church is not an autonomous society, but the mystical complement of her Lord and Saviour, since her identity with him involves total dependence upon, and correspondence with, all that he is. On the other hand, as his mystical complement she is, in this world, his representative and his embodiment, and that in two senses; first, as setting forth before the Father the response of man to God in Christ, and secondly as setting forth before mankind that same response which is 'the obedience of the Christ'.

[1] Rev. 5^{10}, Eph. 2^6.   [2] James 1^{18}.
[3] Jer. 2^3.   [4] 1 Cor. 15$^{20-23}$.
[5] Rom. 8^{23}; cp. 2 Cor. 5^5, Eph. 1$^{13,\ 14}$.

vi

Christian insight into revealed truth is beset by corresponding difficulties, and involves a share in that scandal of the cross which is inseparable from 'the obedience of the Christ'. Implications of 'obedience' and our failure to co-operate therein. Yet, notwithstanding our present imperfection, the church is identified with Jesus in his saving work. Complementary aspects of the 'new creation' theme bear upon problems of the Christian mission.

Mystical union with Christ and participation in the Spirit give to the church a special insight into human nature, its present condition and its destiny, an insight which is capable of penetrating far beyond the horizons of worldly wisdom. For us, as for the seer of the Apocalypse, a door has been opened in heaven. With him we have been admitted to the scene of that adoration which is being offered to God and the Lamb by all orders of creation.[1] Of this three things may be said. In the first place, the insight concerning man which is given in the Christian revelation does not exempt the church from those alternating temptations to presumption and despair which beset our fallen nature in this world. Moreover, Christians are no less liable than other men to become infected with the spiritual maladies which are characteristic of their own age and of their own social environment. Secondly, the insight granted to the church gives a deeper consciousness of disparity between things as they are in the world around us and that state of things which might be brought to pass if God's will were suffered to prevail. The tension so created brings its own peculiar temptations and difficulties of which the complacently secular mind knows nothing. For example the Christian enthusiast for social order may be tempted to lose sight of the heavenly peace in his rightful pursuit of the earthly peace, with consequent loss of vision and lowering of motive power. Or the danger may take a contrary form, as when genuine piety shrinks into the indifferentism of the pietist with respect to social evils.

These difficulties correspond to the fact that the conflict between light and darkness has its centre in the flesh of Jesus, the 'one flesh' with which we are identified in that single mystery

---

[1] Rev. 4, 5, on which see *Dominion*, pp. 195 *f.*

which is Christ and the church.[1] Yet, on the other hand, the tension is matched by a rich endowment of grace. Having 'the firtsfruits of the Spirit' we 'groan within ourselves'.[2] If our partaking of the Spirit creates a deeper nostalgia of dissatisfaction with things as they are in human affairs, it also gives grounds for hope which lie altogether outside the compass of worldly wisdom. Just so far as men share the mind of Christ and experience the power of the Spirit they gain enlarged perspectives which reveal to them deeper dimensions of possibility in human life. Thirdly, as the meeting-place of two worlds, the church regards human problems from a standpoint which must inevitably seem strange and at times even repellent to unregenerate man. The pursuit of the heavenly peace is at once more radical and more comprehensive, more exacting in its demands and more mysterious in its issues, than the pursuit of purely mundane ends can ever be. For that very reason it will always have about it something enigmatic and baffling to those who follow a different path. In the measure in which this otherworldly end is faithfully sought, it will appear to many to be unpractical or unreal. The activities which it inspires will sometimes prove disconcerting, the achievements which stand to its credit disappointing, the motives which it generates incomprehensible.

So much is adumbrated in our Lord's conversation with Nicodemus which leads up to the mysterious statement about the brazen serpent. If the doctrine of the new birth, with its lowly return to the beginning, proves to be a stumbling-block, then the whole community of new-born Christians will inevitably be involved in the scandal.[3] For those who are begotten by the Spirit are led by him into participation in the mystery of Christ's obedience. 'The obedience of the Christ', unfolded in the gospels, is continued in the church.[4] Let us consider what this means. The highest activity for which our nature was designed is one, not of self-assertion, but rather of self-submission. It is not *our* achievement that matters, but rather God's achievement in us. That is effected through our co-operation and involves the exercise of obedience. Now at its highest level obedience does not mean a mere acquiescence in what is ordained,

---

[1] See above, § ii, last par., and *Dominion*, Ch. V, especially p. 136.
[2] Rom. 8[23].
[3] See *Dominion*, pp. 140, 146.   [4] Rom. 5[19], 2 Cor. 10[5].

nor does it necessarily mean an unquestioning acceptance of what is appointed. It is rather the submission of the whole self to God in self-oblation. It is a consecration of all the faculties to the service of God; and this implies a co-ordination of all the capacities of body and mind to that one positive end. In this sense obedience is not so much the foregoing of what we desire, as the bending of all our energies towards what God desires. It is easy to assert ourselves; it is hard, because unnatural, to suppress ourselves. Obedience is in equal contrast to both. For it involves the difficult task of entering into the mind of God in whatever way he may reveal it to us. It involves also a process of sustained response to the revelation given.

Such is the nature of that co-operation to which we are committed by virtue of our incorporation into Christ. The situation is, however, complicated by the fact that the faithfulness with which the heavenly peace is pursued is never complete. Its integrity is always marred by faults of wilfulness, worldliness and the like. In short the scandal and folly of the cross are, in the church of God, strangely mingled with the wholly adverse scandal and folly of human sin. Now if the partnership between Christ and the church were no more than a human relationship of reciprocity, as between two persons of equal status, the presence of sin in the church would be fatal to her mission,—and if so, then also to his. For identity of mission between him and her might seem to involve him in her failure. This identity of mission, however, follows from the mystical identity in 'one flesh', and it is that fact which provides the solution of the dilemma now confronting us. By virtue of that mysterious fact the church embodies the saving mercy of God to a sinful world, as that mercy is bestowed in Christ. As representing her Saviour she is the channel of his saving action, being sent by him as truly as he was sent by the Father. The 'place' of reconciliation with God is the flesh of Jesus in which Christ and the church are one.[1] For this is his crowning act of lowliness, that he, not only reconciles sinners to the Father, but also associates them with himself in the work of reconciliation. This could not be so unless the church were the home of sinners, those very persons whom Jesus received, and for whose sakes he was 'made sin'. As he identified himself with us in our sins, so he identifies us with him

[1] For this phraseology see the note to the last par. of § ii, above.

23

in his victorious act of reparation for sin and in its redemptive consequences for mankind.

In concluding this section let us recall some principal features of the creationist analogy. The mystery of Christ and the church may be summed up in two words, namely *identity* and *co-operation*. Together these two words signify the two complementary aspects of the 'one flesh'. Each represents a fundamental aspect of revealed truth. Yet neither can be fully understood in its implications apart from the other. Here the reader is in possession of a leading clue to the remaining argument of this treatise, of which a main topic can now be briefly indicated. As, in the story of rebellion, Eve was the human agent through whom Adam's disobedience infected all, so in the story of redemption the new Eve is the human agent through whom the obedience of the new Adam becomes effectual in all. This truth has more than one possible application. Here we will keep to that aspect which is most directly relevant to our argument. A question with which we shall be continually occupied in the present work may be stated thus: In what sense can we believe that the obedience of the Christ, as head of creation, becomes effectual in mankind through the agency of the church? Clearly the question and its answer will have a close connexion with the previously mentioned function of the church as the representative of her Lord in setting forth his obedience to the Father before God and man.[1]

vii

The manifestation of Christ's obedience in the church effected through a transformation in us which corresponds to his transfiguration. That gospel event symbolized the unity of revelation in the all-inclusive Christ mystery to which the church belongs. So the transfiguration is re-enacted in the church with a significantly detailed parallelism; e.g. a foreshadowing of final glory in our present mortal flesh.

To the far-reaching question posed at the end of the last section an answer must now be provisionally stated, so far as possible, in a form suggested by scripture. In the first place,

[1] See above, the concluding sentence of § v.

then, the obedience of the Christ can become known to sinners only so far as it is manifested in and through persons who represent, and in some sense embody, that obedience. Now the church, as the firstfruits of creation in Christ, is the sphere where men become partakers in the obedience of the Christ. But since all men are sinners the manifestation is inevitably made through sinful agents. What then is manifested through this medium? Clearly not a display of human perfections, but rather a transformation of the unholy into the holy. In the new creation the direction of human life has been changed once and for all. But also, its direction is continuously being changed. At this point we may hope to clarify more fully the implications of a phrase previously used; for the temple of Christ's body is the place of transfiguration.[1] It is, perhaps, no accident that in the Epistle to the Romans St Paul introduces the practical application of his argument with a precept which has verbal affinity with the gospel story of the transfiguration. In 12[2] he bids his readers to be '*transformed* by the renewal of the mind'. The word here italicized is used by both St Mark and St Matthew in the phrase: 'he was *transfigured* before them.'[2] Whether consciously or unconsciously, the apostle here bears witness to a real affinity between the mystery of our Lord's transfiguration and the whole character of the Christian life.

One important aspect of this suggested affinity could be stated thus: As the transfiguration of Jesus both manifested and foreshadowed the single mystery of his death and resurrection, so the transfigured lives of his people manifest in the world the power of that same mystery of death and resurrection, and also foreshadow its ultimate effects for all mankind. The scriptural development of this theme, however, is many-sided and far reaching, as has been indicated elsewhere.[3] In the New Testament there is an integration of all mysteries of revelation into one; amongst these the existence of the church is included in the one all-embracing mystery of the new creation. Moreover, in

[1] See above, § ii, last par., and note.

[2] Mark 9[2], Matt. 17[2]. A similar instance may be cited from Rev. 7[14]. where the *whitened* garments of the saints in bliss correspond to the white garments of the transfigured Jesus, 'such as no fuller on earth can *whiten* them' (Mark 9[3]).

[3] e.g., in this Chapter, § iv, par. 4, last sentence with note and par. 5; also § v, par. 2, last sentence with note.

the previous volume it was pointed out that for the evangelists the transfiguration of our Lord is the event which symbolized this integral character of the new creation. This it did in two respects: first by foreshadowing the death and resurrection as together forming one mystery, and secondly by showing the fulfilment of the old covenant as a whole in this single mystery. These two implications of the event gave it the character of a focussing point for the whole of revelation, and even more—a concrete embodiment of the truth that in the Christ there is a recapitulation of all things (Ephesians 1 10).

If then the body of Christ is the temple or shrine in which we are worshippers, it is for us also 'the place of transfiguration', that is the place wherein the unholy are transformed into the holy. It follows that, by virtue of our identity with Jesus in the 'one flesh', the mystery of his transfiguration is in some sense re-enacted in his church. But further, as 'we are a kind of first-fruits of his creatures' this same mystery of the transfigured Christ is ever sending forth beams of light through the church to reach and penetrate the 'all flesh' of mankind in whom the incarnate Word has tabernacled.[1] Thus it follows that the whole 'mystery of the Christ' is re-enacted in the church in a manner which corresponds to the transfiguration scene. As the glory for which man was predestined in the plan of creation is restored in Jesus through his fulfilment of Israel's vocation to sacrificial obedience, so also in the church Jesus is transfigured in his members by their participation with him in this vocation. The parallel, however, goes deeper still. We recall the fact that the transfiguration was not the fruition of glory, but its anticipation. The glory on the mount was a foregleam of that greater splendour which belongs to the resurrection. For it is only in the risen life that the fruits of sacrifice are fully garnered. Moreover, the mystery was manifested in the flesh of Jesus during his state of humiliation, and was seen only by the chosen witnesses.

These aspects of our Lord's transfiguration reappear in the life of the church. The mystery taking place now in Christ's mystical body on earth is a foreshadowing of that final glory which is to be unveiled in the general resurrection at the last day. It is indeed a real anticipation. We are already bathed in the transfiguring rays of light which stream forth from the Sun of

[1] cp. *Dominion*, pp. 135 *f.*

Righteousness. For where his light enters, even in this vale of tears, there is already the dawn of the eternal day. Yet we are still in the world, as Jesus once was. In our earthly pilgrimage, as in his earthly life, the glory is hidden under the weakness of the flesh; and yet, as then so now, it is also unveiled to the eye of faith. This parallelism has, inevitably, certain consequences in us, as in him. 'As he is, so are we in this world.' The 'we' stands midway between the two halves of this text; and each half of the truth stated is of equal importance. We share the glory of Jesus, and are being transformed into his likeness. But the transforming process traces out in us the pattern which by faith we now see in him because that same pattern was once traced out in his mortal flesh. All that he was is now included in what he is, and must therefore be reproduced in us. This is indicated by St Paul when he speaks of our 'being *conformed* to his death', and then, in the next paragraph declares that the Saviour will 'refashion the body of our humiliation to be *conformed* to the body of his glory'. Here the transfiguring process is seen to be one which brings us into the identical 'form' which belongs to the mystery of Christ's death and resurrection.[1]

viii

The new tabernacle and the new Israel. Jesus and his church together 'on the mount' and 'in the wilderness'. In our access to the heavenly sanctuary of a new Jerusalem we are 'strangers and pilgrims' in the world; and this involves a 'discipline of sons'. Vision and hope on the mountain top. The inclusive and integral character of restoration in the new creation, where also the inward and outward aspects of the transformation are complementary.

The glory of the only Son making his lowly response to the Father is still manifested as of old. Now, as then, it is manifested in that fleshly tabernacle which he made so completely his own that in it we are one with him.[2] So, in the 'one flesh' of this tabernacle the church is the place where we enter into the obedi-

---

[1] Phil. 3[10, 21]. Moreover, the language of *con*formation is complementary to that of *trans*formation which, as we have seen, was employed in Rom. 12[2].

[2] For this and what follows see *Dominion*, Ch. V, §§ i and ii, especially pp. 135*f.*

ence of the Christ. Not only *for* us, but also *in* us, the sanctuary of our Saviour's flesh is the place of sacrifice, so that the glory of the Shekinah and the flame of the burnt-offering are one. The church, therefore, is the camp of Israel in the wilderness of a fallen world; and the standards of this camp move forward along the one track by which alone men can come to the promised land. Now in the far-off beginnings of redemptive history the wilderness beneath the mount was the place where the covenant was made, and where the tabernacle was first set up. Accordingly, in the prophetic view, this was the place of the divine espousals, where Israel was vowed to her true allegiance and became the mystic bride of deity.[1] So too the wilderness was the place to which Israel must be recalled for spiritual renewal, the place of purification and reconciliation for those who have breathed the poisonous air of an idolatrous civilization.[2] All this provides a background to the transfiguration scene in the gospels, where the flesh of Jesus is plainly identified with the new tabernacle[3] with one important difference to which we must now give consideration.

In the story of Israel at the mount of God the tabernacle was set up on the level plain beneath the mount, whereas in the gospel story the new tabernacle of transfigured humanity is seen, *not beneath but, upon the mount*; and this fact has a twofold significance. As we have seen, it foreshadows exaltation and glory to come through the mystery of death and resurrection. But, secondly, it also signifies the situation of the chosen witnesses who represent the new Israel. Like Moses and Elijah they have access to the presence of God; but they find that presence now in the Shekinah glory of the beloved Son. Like Moses and Elijah, however, they find the presence upon the mount in detachment from the world below. Nevertheless Jesus himself entered the wilderness of this world; and in the original story the mount is situated in the wilderness. It seems, therefore, that, although the place of access to the new tabernacle is 'on the mount', it may, from another point of view, be considered to be also 'in the wilderness'.[4] When we pass from 'the wilderness' to the holy land the theme of 'the mount' undergoes a further development.

---

[1] Jer. 2[2].   [2] cp. *Dominion*, Ch. II, § i.
[3] See *Apostolic Ministry*, pp. 86 *ff*, and *Dominion*, pp. 168 *f*.
[4] For which see further the next paragraph.

'The mountain of the Lord's house' at Jerusalem was alternately the centre upon which the prophets fixed their hopes and again the object of their despair.[1] In the end our Lord referred to it as 'this mountain', a mere obstruction to be removed by the power of unwavering faith.[2]

In prophetic pictures, however, the imagery of the tabernacle is sometimes applied to the sanctuary at Jerusalem, as though the contrast between the wilderness and the holy land were destined to disappear.[3] This fusion of types becomes normal in the New Testament, although the treatment is varied.[4] It takes a special form in the Epistle to the Hebrews, where the obedience of our high priest is offered in and through his flesh in the heavenly tabernacle;—where also, by their compresence with him, his people are identified with him in his offering. Here the place of the new cultus is situated upon 'Mount Zion' in the heavenly Jerusalem; and our immediate access to it is contrasted with the barriers which fenced off the mount of God in the wilderness (12^{18-24}). Moreover it is clear that a profound significance attaches to this conception of the heavenly tabernacle. It is because we are one with Jesus, our priest-king, in the sanctuary of a heavenly city that we are also, of necessity, 'strangers and pilgrims' in this present world like the patriarchs of old (Hebrews 11^{13}). Moreover, for those who are identified with the glory of Christ's obedience this fallen world has, in itself, nothing substantial to offer. Apart from that glory and all that it signifies this world is just a wilderness, a place without resources or interest, in which homeless wanderers may pitch their tents, as their Lord once did.[5]

The author of the epistle is, in effect, saying that if we share Christ's dominion we must drink the cup of his sacrifice. Just so far as we show forth the obedience by which Adam's dominion was restored, we must do so in detachment from a world which knows not that law. Because we belong to the heavenly sanc-

---

[1] Isa. $2^{1\it{ff}}$, Mic. $4^{1\it{ff}}$, Jer. 7^{1-16}, Ezek. 8–11, 40–47, Zech. 8^3.

[2] Mark 11^{23}.

[3] cp. Isa. 4^{2-6}, Ezek. 37^{21-28}. See also Ecclus. 24^{3-11} (Exod. 13^{21}, $14^{19, 24}$, etc.) and Wisd. 9^8, which makes Solomon's temple a copy of the eternal tabernacle (Exod. 25^{40}; cp. Heb. $8^{2, 5}$).

[4] And in St John's gospel unique. See the final note to § ii above; and cp. Rev. 7^{15} and 1 Pet. 4^{14} with the body-temple image elsewhere.

[5] *Dominion*, Ch. V, § i.

tuary, where the filial response of the only-begotten Son is offered to the Father, we must needs embrace that discipline of sons which is proper to a journey through the wilderness.[1] We must, therefore, go forth from the camp of things-as-they-are to Jesus, our forerunner, 'bearing his reproach', even as 'the reproach of the Christ' once took Moses into the wilderness (13^{12-14}, 11^{24-29}). Because we are even now entering, through his righteousness, into the messianic rest or peace ($4^{3,\ 11}$, 7^2), therefore 'we have not here a continuing city, but seek that which is to come' (13^{14}; cp. 11^{8-16}).

The heavenly sanctuary is 'upon the mount'; and this fact presents one further aspect for our consideration. From the mountain top the wilderness can be seen for what it is, in its full extent of waste. Thus our Lord saw it from his high vantage ground, when, like the serpent in the wilderness, he was 'lifted up' on the cross. But also, from the mountain top other landscapes come into view, as when Moses from Mount Pisgah saw spread out before him the whole land of promise. So, too, the otherworldly vision of those who worship in the heavenly tabernacle is, in the measure of its detachment, the less likely to be deceived by the *mirage* under which the desert of this fallen world conceals its barren wastes. Moreover, this negative realism is not to be confused with the cynical despair of the disillusioned. For it is the counterpart of a lively faith that God will make good the final redemption of his handiwork in creation.[2] We have 'tasted the good word of God and the powers of the age to come'.[3] We can neither doubt that word nor set limits to those powers. In the New Testament they are represented as working from within outwards. If Christ's body is the place of transfiguration, it is also true that the material now subjected to the transforming power of the gospel includes at least the whole of humanity, whether men be conscious of this fact or not.

Even this, however, falls short of the truth. For the process at work in the new creation issues from the restoration of Adam's dominion in Christ. It includes, therefore, not only the return of man to the path of obedience, but also the return of all creation through man to the plan of the Creator's design. To that plan belongs the effective disposal of nature's resources under a

[1] Heb. 12^{1-13}; and see last note.
[2] cp. Rom. 8^{18} *ff*. [3] Heb. 6^5.

faithful human stewardship—a stewardship so exercised that the creation is redeemed from waste and barrenness, and thus rendered productive and fruitful. This co-operation of man, however, is consistent with the truth that the great transformation is the work of God himself; for it is man's return to obedience which enables God to act. This is the constant theme of the prophets in those pictures of nature transfigured with which they anticipate the new creation. If the divine judgements upon sin caused to 'come up briers and thorns', yet this was to last only 'until the Spirit be poured out from on high and the wilderness become a fruitful field'. Then 'the wilderness and the solitary place shall be glad; and the desert shall rejoice and blossom as the rose'.[1] In the New Testament the fulfilment of these promises begins. Thus it is that the healing miracles are clearly regarded as signs of the integral character of salvation in the new creative era which has dawned.[2]

A redemption which is universal must not only include all within its range; it must also penetrate the whole of the material included. The restoration of the Creator's design in the universe includes the healing of human nature; and this, in turn, implies the integration of the whole man including the body, which in Hebrew thought represents the whole man. Moreover to the body appertains also its material environment. Lastly, if it be true that the redemptive process works outward from within, this cannot be taken to mean that we may disregard the outward transformation until the interior process is complete. For the transformation of man's interior life is completed only through its outward expression in the body; and just so far as such outward expression is not achieved, this failure reacts unfavourably. On the one hand the interior life is certainly restricted and impoverished in effective scope and in self-evidencing power; and on the other hand the transforming effects of the gospel are, to that extent, not objectively manifested in Christian witness to the world. The right combination of contrasts here reviewed will provide matter for further consideration at a later stage.

[1] Isa. 32$^{13, 15}$, 35$^{1\,ff}$; cp. 49$^{8-13}$, 55$^{6-13}$.
[2] Full details are given in *Dominion*, Chs. I and II.

CHAPTER II

THE CITY OF GOD

i

The contrast between the tower of Babel and the New Jerusalem in a wider biblical setting (Philippians 2[5-11]). The rejected stone, the new name and the 'building' of the New Eve. Relation of the church, as bride, to the city of God to be determined by reference to 'the obedience of the Christ'.

In the tower of Babel St Augustine found a biblical type for that order of human life which he called 'the earthly city', and which he contrasted with 'the city of God'.[1] In the New Testament the true antithesis of Babel is seen in the New Jerusalem. But also, the contrasts between these two entities have a wider biblical background. In the story of Babel the builders say: 'let us get us a name.' They build for their own glory, to gratify their pride in achievement. In the New Jerusalem, on the other hand, the name of God is upon the foreheads of his worshippers. They exist, not for themselves, but for him who is the only builder of the city. The contrast here is parallel to that between the figures respectively of Adam and Christ in St Paul's great statement (Philippians 2[5-11]). For Adam grasped at the name and honour of God by yielding to the serpent's suggestion: 'Ye shall be as God.' To this picture of a man grasping at equality with God correspond the tower of Babel and its builders with their ambitious project of reaching up to heaven. Christ, however, did not reach up, but came down. He did not grasp at glory, but surrendered it. Whereas the first Adam took what was not his, the second Adam poured out his all unto death. For this act of obedience he received the divine name of 'Lord' as the counterpart of his human name, Jesus.[2] He did not exalt himself to heaven, but was exalted thither by the Father.

---

[1] See *Dominion*, p. 80 with note 1.
[2] cp. above, Ch. I, § v, par. 5, final note.

As Babel's origin can be traced, in the biblical narrative, to the suggestion of the serpent and to the transgression of Adam, so the city of the new creation has God for its builder and has no other foundation than Jesus. The stone which the earthly builders rejected in favour of their own plans was found to have the chief place in the heavenly builder's design. The rejection of this stone was predestined from the beginning and is already symbolically anticipated in the story of Babel. For Jesus is the site of both creations, and 'other foundation can no man lay'. Accordingly the slaying of the heavenly Lamb was already decreed when the false foundations of 'the earthly city' were first rebelliously laid. On the other hand the founding of God's city upon the rejected stone is linked by St Peter in the Acts ($4^{11,\ 12}$) with a declaration that salvation is through the name of Jesus alone. Entrance into that holy land whose centre is the new Jerusalem belongs only to those who follow the new Joshua,[1] and who live by the faith that Jesus is Lord. The stone and the name have a like significance.[2] The security and peace of the new city rest upon all that Jesus is as the crucified Lord, the lowly one whom the Father exalted, rejected indeed of men, but accepted by God. As the earthly city took its rise (on earth) from Adam's disobedience, so the New Jerusalem was founded upon that obedience which Jesus rendered even unto death.

In the story of the first creation the word used to describe the fashioning of Eve out of Adam's side means literally 'to build'.[3] So when the second Adam fell asleep in death upon the cross and his newly opened side became the site of the new creation, God built once more a new Eve. She also, like her prototype, is 'the mother of all living'.[4] For, as St Paul reminds us, 'Jerusalem that is above is our mother',[5] that is, the mother of all who live in Jesus. Thus, the scene of the Lamb's death on Calvary, in which St John finds this further mystery enacted, has for its counterpart the vision of the New Jerusalem in the Revelation, where the holy city is identified with 'the bride, the wife of the Lamb'. This identification of the city with the bride brings us face to face with a question which, so to speak,

---

[1] Whose name rendered into Greek became 'Jesus'.

[2] A verbal connexion between them may have been found in Zech. 3^9.

[3] Gen. 2^{22}; cp. RV margin. For what follows see above § v, par. 5, and cp. 2 Esdras, Ch. $10^{25\,ff,\ 40\,ff}$.

[4] Gen. 3^{20}.   [5] Gal. 4^{26}.

D   33

has already raised its head, both in the present volume and in its predecessor. The visible church is the bride of Christ and therefore has real identity with God's city. But the sense in which this identification may be rightly affirmed requires very careful discrimination. This fact has been variously indicated throughout these volumes concerning *The Form of the Servant*. It is, for example, bound up with the problem concerning the complementary character of the two creations.

The church is the firstfruits of redeemed humanity, but also the spearhead of Christ's continuing conflict with evil.[1] She is, to say the least, the present embodiment and pledge of Christ's kingdom, and the appointed organ, in and through which the reign of God in Christ is even now taking control of human life. But the church is also the camp of Israel in the wilderness, the scene of our present battle with the serpent, the mount of vision and transfiguration from which we view a promised land not yet entered. Once more, she is the place of travail, where, having the firstfruits of the Spirit, we endure the birthpangs of a new age as we await the redemption of our body through death and resurrection.[2] In short, to sum up, the church is the place where men and women become partakers in the obedience of the Christ. That obedience has already provided one of the main threads running through previous stages of our argument. We have seen that it connects the sacrifice of the Lamb of God with his victorious restoration of Adam's dominion, and, again, that the church, as the new Eve and mystic bride who participates both in the sacrifice and in the restoration, is united with both of these mysteries in the one all-embracing mystery of the new creation. Moreover, as the bride of the Lamb, the church is also identified with the New Jerusalem. Accordingly our next step must be to consider the characteristics of the city of God as determined by its conformity to 'the obedience of the Christ'.

ii

The 'descending city' a theological mystery, transcending, yet entering history. Its relation to the event of the Incarnation, and

---

[1] cp. *Dominion*, Ch. V, § 1.

[2] Rom 8$^{18-23}$; see also below, Ch. V, § v, last two pars.

its function in a transformed creation. Integral relation of the
holy city to the sacrifice and to the victory of the Lamb. As
present bearer of the Lamb, his bride has identity with him in the
new creation process. Revelation 21[1-3] shows the fulfilment of the
Emmanuel prophecy, God *with* us.

The New Jerusalem, as described in the Revelation of St
John, has three characteristics which at this point claim our
attention. Let us take them in the order in which the seer saw
them in his vision. First, the holy city is seen 'descending out of
heaven from God'.[1] Secondly, in the city God and the Lamb
are the temple, and the Lamb is the lamp through which the
glory of God gives light. Thirdly, in the city's light the nations
walk, and into her the kings of the earth bring their glory and
honour. All these three points, as we shall see, have their
counterparts in the mystery of the obedience of the Christ.
There is, also, one further observation to be made concerning
the general character of such visions. In the present instance the
New Jerusalem belongs to the New Age, wherein a new heaven
and a new earth have come into existence. The manifestation is,
in one sense, timeless. For the scenes in the Revelation appear
to be primarily dramatic representations of theological mysteries
which do not necessarily show a precise sequence of events.
Nevertheless the new age arrived with the coming of the Christ,
and by his victorious ascent to heaven he recreated the heavenly
order. For then the defeated dragon with his host was cast down
from on high.[2] But further, by this cosmic victory Jesus re-
created the whole universe, so that, despite the vicissitudes of
history, 'a new earth' is already in being.

This last statement, however, requires fuller elucidation. In
terms of a sequence of events the descent of the New Jerusalem
might be conceived to have its starting-point in the descent of
the Spirit at Pentecost. Yet here we must be prepared to recognize both a parallel and a contrast as between Jesus and his
bride. The Lamb of God is he who 'came down out of heaven',[3]
and the bride of the Lamb also comes down 'out of heaven'.
Jesus came from God; and the holy city has the same origin.

---

[1] Rev. 21[2, 10]. Further details: in v. 2 'prepared as a bride adorned for her
husband';—in v. 10 'having the glory of God'.
[2] Rev. 12.   [3] John 3[13]; cp. 6[38], etc.

But the Lamb descended once for all, whereas the city is seen in process of descent. Here, perhaps, we have an indication that the whole picture of the New Jerusalem belongs to a mystical order of reality which transcends time and history, but which, nonetheless, is continuously entering into and working upon the events of the Christian dispensation. This view would, in the context, give further significance to the mention of 'a new earth'.[1] For the Incarnation has left nothing unchanged in this creation. Moreover, the portent of the New Jerusalem descending from heaven to earth is itself an abiding fact of the Christian centuries which has transformed the face of things and will continue to do so.

In the vision of the descending city we may also see another truth expressed. The Son of Man came from heaven. His coming was a condescension in uttermost lowliness to the level of this our earthly scene. That was the essence of his obedience. He did not climb up; he came down. His descent signified his humble submission to the Father's will—that submission which was the heart of his sacrifice as the predestined Lamb of God. Now the holy city derives its whole character from the Lamb. It descends 'prepared as a bride adorned for her husband'. Its brilliant luminary is none other than the Lamb himself. Its descent, therefore, is something more than a sequel to the Lamb's descent. For the whole glory of his sacrifice is present in the descending city. It is this alone which gives to the city its character as the New Jerusalem. But further, the city descends out of the new heaven. Its downward movement is a process of the new creation inaugurated by the Lamb's victory, and integral with that victory. The triumph of the Lamb is the heavenly fruition of his obedience; and the essence of his obedience was manifested in his lowly descent by which the glory of God was made accessible to man. So too, the city, as the bride of the Lamb, has identity of life with him; and therefore the pattern of his lowly descent is renewed in her. As she comes down the obedience of the Christ is being manifested as vitally operative and effective towards mankind.

In our exposition of the truths implicit in this representation there is one further step to be taken. The descending city is the bearer of the Lamb. It is no mere figurative portrayal of the

[1] Rev. 21[1].

Lamb, but the Lamb himself who is present in his bride, as she was once present in him in the days of his mortal flesh.[1] So in her descent he also descends. As she comes down, he becomes accessible to earth, and that too in the glory of his sacrifice. The new creation is one in all its parts. The new earth began to be when the Word became flesh. The new heaven is where the Lamb reigns victoriously in that same flesh. The new heaven and the new earth are united in the descending city which brings the tabernacle of God down to be 'with men'. It is worth noticing that this sequence corresponds to the order of Revelation 21[1-3]: (1) the new heaven and the new earth; (2) the descending city; (3) the tabernacle of God with men. The emphatic echo here of the Emmanuel prophecy—'God *with* us'[2]—is complementary (but, as we have seen, not contradictory) to the 'God *in* us' of St John's prologue,[3] Men must approach the city, if they are to walk in its light. They must enter it freely, if they are to bring into it their glory and honour. This is precisely what the seer saw them doing. So we come to the third feature of the vision which we singled out for consideration. With it we pass to a new stage of this inquiry, as we return once more to the question: In what sense can we believe that the obedience of the Christ, as head of creation, becomes effectual in mankind through the church?

iii

By entry into the holy city we return to the uncreated light to which we belong. Its focus is the sacrificial flame of perfect obedience radiating from the Lamb of God. Our access to that flame is a participation in his obedience. Its positive character involves free co-operation of all our powers, redeemed from misuse to be vehicles of his action in the world. The city, the leaven and the mustard seed. The parallel with the latter shows the paradox of divine lowliness.

It is to be remembered that all men were created to enjoy the uncreated light which is the glory of God. Indeed, as the light of

---

[1] See above, Ch. I, § iii, par. 3, and § iv, pars. 3 and 4.

[2] The 'with' is repeated three times in Rev. 21[3]; and this corresponds to Isa. 7[14], with the Greek rendering of 'Emmanuel' in Isa. 8[8, 10] (LXX).

[3] See *Dominion*, p. 135 with note 4.

37

God's grace it is our true home from which we have wandered away. To it we return once more by entering the holy city which is the bride of Christ. The glory is made accessible to the dwellers in the city because the Lamb, incarnate, crucified and risen, is the human lamp in which the divine glory is concentrated, and from which its light streams forth. Moreover, the Lamb is the lamp because he is the sacrificial victim in whom the true obedience of man, once for all offered to God the Father, can be seen. The flame of the sacrifice, rising to the heavenly Father from his incarnate Son, makes the city to be the very hearth of God,[1] where his children may gather and find their true peace. The citizens walking in the light of that flame are bathed in it and transfigured by it. Thus they become objects of light and bearers of the sacrificial flame.[2] They are partakers in the obedience of the Christ. Here we must recall the fact that the obedience which Jesus rendered to the Father was active and positive. Outwardly, in the hours of his passion, he was passive in the hands of sinners. But inwardly he was master of the situation; for he was doing the Father's will. *They* were caught in the toils of their own waywardness, whereas *he*, with serene deliberation, was fulfilling his destiny.

This obedience which is the substance of Christ's sacrifice is made accessible to mankind in the church, where it has a like character. Accordingly the obedience by which men live in the city of God is not a mere abnegation of human powers; it is rather a consecration of all human resources to the service of God.[3] Such consecration involves something much more radical and exacting than is commonly understood by the word 'obedience'. The child at school or the enlisted soldier may be required to obey commands without reasons being given; and such unquestioning obedience has its place in human life. Yet such examples do not suggest the deeper possibilities which are included in the biblical meaning of obedience. Such possibilities are indicated by our Lord's words in St John's Gospel concerning the differences between a mere slave-service and the co-operation of friends: 'The slave knoweth not what his Lord doeth; but I have called you friends.'[4] To partake in the obedience of the Christ means that we are permitted to share his mind

---

[1] Isa. 29[1].   [2] cp. 2 Cor. 4[6, 7].
[3] cp. above, Ch. I, § vi, par. 3.   [4] John 15[15].

as he makes it known to us. For only thus can our obedience be, like his, the consecration of every faculty to the service of God; and if we are to do God's will we must 'understand what the will of the Lord is'.[1] Only by entering into the mind of Christ can we hope to understand his purpose and to recognize the means by which he is carrying that purpose into effect. Only so far as we attain to such understanding can we co-operate fruitfully with our Lord in that freewill offering which he made upon Calvary.

Thus the co-operation of the new Eve with the obedience of the new Adam is a participation in his sacrifice which has a correspondingly costing character. The end of true sacrifice, however, is not death but life, not negation but affirmation. This we have already seen in our interpretation of Christ's sacrifice as a single mystery which has two aspects, inasmuch as it includes both death and resurrection.[2] So, when human resources are genuinely submitted to the will of God as revealed in the mind of Christ, then by virtue of their dedication those resources are transformed into something new. They are taken up into the redemptive process of the new creation. This transformation has two aspects, the one negative and the other positive. For first, human powers so dedicated are themselves redeemed from distortion, disintegration and waste which are the nemesis of their misappropriation to sinful uses. Secondly, being rescued from the barren activities of self-will, these human powers are restored to their true purpose. They become serviceable to God in the furthering of his redemptive plan for creation. They become part of the materials of our Lord's sacrifice, means through which the efficacy of that sacrifice is rendered vitally operative in the world. This is the process described in the vision. The city which bears the Lamb downwards from heaven to earth is not a closed entity; its gates are always open. So the downward movement of the city is met by an upward movement of mankind, as through the open gates men bring the glory and honour of the nations into the sanctuary.

A theological mystery cannot become fully explicit in a pictorial representation. So the vision of the New Jerusalem suggests much which it does not unfold. It sets before us the true goal of human life as a present reality already fully existent.

_____

[1] Eph. 5[17].   [2] cp. above, Ch. I, § ii, par. 4.

This reality ever transcends our world; yet it is ever coming to fulfilment in the order of being which Christ inaugurated. That new order can be likened to leaven working in the lump of the old order, as our Lord plainly indicated.[1] On the other hand, in another parable the new order was likened to a mustard seed which became a tree and gave shelter to the birds of the heaven. Here, as in the vision of the New Jerusalem, the peoples of the world were gathered into the true Israel of God.[2] Both images (the city and the tree) suggest the idea of 'Christendom'—that is, an order of society in which the rule of Christ is so effectually realized that 'the glory and honour of the nations', in entering that order, are conformed to that rule; in short, they would seem to imply an order of life in which all the good gifts of God in creation are redeemed from misuse and remoulded to a Christian form. Between our Lord's parable and the seer's vision another kind of similarity appears which also deserves consideration.

The parallel lies in a certain correspondence of contrasts. The size of the mustard plant is in inverse proportion to that of the seed from which it sprang. Its eventual greatness is in contrast to the smallness of its original form. So, too, it gives shelter to the birds of the heaven only after its seed has been cast into the earth. Similarly, in the vision, the proud wealth of the nations is laid at the feet of the meek and lowly Lamb; and the earth-dwellers go up to heavenly glory, only because the heavenly city comes down to earth. Both images suggest the gracious lowliness of God's love in condescending to man in order to enfold and embrace him, and thereby to raise him toward heaven. Moreover, this divine, yet lowly, embrace has taken concrete form in and through the obedience of the Christ, symbolized, on the one hand, by the sowing of the insignificant mustard seed and, on the other hand, by the descent of the city

---

[1] 'The kingdom of heaven is like unto leaven' (Matt. 13[33]). This corresponds to the symbolism of Lev. 23[15-17], where on the feast of Pentecost two leavened loaves were offered as firstfruits unto the Lord. So in the fulfilment (Acts 2) we see a richer pentecostal offering where the bread of our humanity has been leavened by the outpoured Spirit.

[2] As in Ezek. 17[22-24], on which see my comment in the *Apostolic Ministry*, p. 73, note 4. There the tender *yōnêk* becomes a great tree, whereas in Dan. 4[10] the sinister Babylonian tree is great from the first. So it is no true parallel, notwithstanding the echo of Ezekiel's phrase about the birds.

bearing the Lamb to earth. Together the two pictures show (the one implicitly, the other explicitly) that the divine embrace of mankind is effected in and through the new Israel, the body and bride of Christ. The parable refers to the single mystery of the Christ in its wholeness; and with this conclusion agrees his loving appreciation of a disciple's faith, though it be as small as a grain of mustard seed (Luke 17⁶).

iv

Relation of the church on earth to the New Jerusalem. Like a Roman colony, it is a frontier post enjoying heavenly citizenship. This again corresponds to the analogy with the transfiguration scene, where in a present setting of lowliness ultimate glory is unveiled. In the 'one flesh' of Jesus conflict continues still; and the entire Christ mystery is mysteriously actualized in its mortal part.

The course of the argument now requires that we should come to closer grips with the question as to what precisely is the relationship in which the church visible here on earth stands to the heavenly Jerusalem. One answer to this question appeared in the last chapter, where the symbolism of the heavenly tabernacle in the Epistle to the Hebrews suggested that, precisely because we are already present with Jesus in the sanctuary of the heavenly Jerusalem, we are for that very reason strangers and pilgrims in this present world, and therefore also subject to that discipline of sons which is proper to a journey through the wilderness.[1] Another way of describing this relationship was put forward by St Paul in his letter to the Philippians. Philippi was a Roman colony. It was therefore a miniature representation of Rome in a distant province of the empire. Moreover, like the apostle himself, some of the Philippians would actually be Roman citizens who enjoyed special privileges wherever the emperor's authority prevailed. Now, as Philippi was a colony of Rome, so the Christian church in Philippi might be regarded as a colony of that heavenly commonwealth which in another letter St Paul had called 'Jerusalem that is above, which is our mother'.[2] Moreover, as members of the church in Philippi, not

---

[1] See above, Ch. I, § viii, pars. 3 and 4.
[2] Gal. 4²⁶.

41

some but all the Christians of that locality were to be regarded as enrolled citizens of the heavenly Jerusalem.[1]

As the Roman citizens in Philippi were truly citizens of their mother-city, Rome, though not present there in person, so also the Christians of Philippi were truly citizens of the heavenly Jerusalem, although in the flesh of their mortal bodies they still sojourned as exiles in a strange land.[2] The Philippian church was like a frontier post of the heavenly country, exhibiting the life and manners of God's city in a world of strangers who knew them not. In his statement, however, the apostle refers to '*our* citizenship', identifying himself with the Philippian Christians. The application of his words cannot, therefore, be restricted to them alone. When he says that 'our commonwealth (or citizenship) is in heaven' he means that the whole visible church on earth is but a colony of that vaster mystery, the true city of God, the bride of Christ. This conception of the church militant as a frontier post of the heavenly country further illustrates our thesis that the whole mystery of the Christ is re-enacted in the church in a manner which corresponds to the transfiguration scene.[3] As surely as the meaning of Roman citizenship was exemplified in distant colonies of the empire, so surely is the visible church the earthly sphere in which the obedience of the Christ is manifested in its true significance. For the church militant, despite its blemishes, is a microcosm of that change in the direction of human life which Christ effected once for all. The visible church, like the sacraments, is an effectual sign of Christ's present glory and of man's high destiny in him.

It will be remembered, however, that the transfiguration was, in form, unlike the resurrection which it symbolized and foreshadowed. So, too, the lowly tabernacle in the wilderness with its surrounding camp foreshadowed the more noble temple in the holy city of Jerusalem. Likewise the glory of the risen body was prefigured on the mount in the transfigured lowliness of the mortal body, the one divine-human Lord being the substance of both mysteries. After the same fashion the visible church has identity with the heavenly Jerusalem of which here on earth that church is the effectual sign. It is precisely *in* the low estate of the

---

[1] Phil. 3[20]; and cp. Phil. 4[3] with Luke 10[20] and Rev. 21[27].

[2] Which gives point to the sequence of Phil. 3[20, 21].

[3] Above, Ch. I, § vii, and below, last par. of this section.

church on earth that the glory of the heavenly city is present and operative. Indeed, it is only so far as the visible church is one with Jesus in the humiliation of his mortal flesh that this lowly camp of Israel in the wilderness can signify and truly manifest the splendours of the New Jerusalem, those splendours which already surround the ascended Lord, and amidst which he will hereafter manifest himself to all. The truths here set forth are symbolized in the seer's vision by the fact that the holy city is seen descending from heaven to earth. For the glory of God's city is the glory of God's condescending love which becomes accessible to us only under the lowly form of the Lamb, and therefore only in and through the low estate of the visible church. As the victorious Lamb retains the marks of his shameful death in his risen glory, so the heavenly Zion where he dwells is fittingly manifested on earth in the mortal flesh of us poor wayfaring sinners.

Thus the low estate of the visible church is signified, not only by the descent of the city, but also by the presence of the Lamb within the descending city. For the Lamb is he who bears the marks of crucifixion in his risen body. In previous statements we have seen that the flesh of Jesus is the site of our present conflict in the church on earth, and again that Jesus did not leave his mortal flesh behind at death but took it with him into the new life when he entered his risen glory.[1] To approach the Lamb by entering the city is, therefore, the same thing as to approach the flesh of Jesus which is the sphere of our earthly conflict. To enter the city is all one with entering into the obedience of the Christ through participation in his sacrifice. Moreover, those who enter the city of God come to it from 'the earthly city' where dwell the fallen children of Adam. To enter the heavenly city, therefore, is to challenge the powers of darkness. For the glory and honour of the nations have fallen under the dragon's power in his usurped kingdom. The treasures of the first creation can be brought within the holy city only by a challenge to that false authority; and it is this inescapable challenge to the usurper which takes place perennially in the church militant, where the conflict of Christ's flesh is unceasingly renewed.

At this point we shall do well to recall what was said previously about the sense in which the visions in the Revelation of

---

[1] See Ch. I, § ii, fourth and last pars. with final note.

43

St John transcend time and history so that their symbolic sequence cannot be exhaustively identified with a given historical sequence at one particular point of time.[1] Of course this general principle of interpretation will have very various implications in different instances. An illustration is provided by what has been said in the preceding paragraph. In the dramatic sequence of the Revelation the entry of the nations into the city, like the actual descent of the city, is subsequent to the final overthrow of the dragon. For the complete manifestation of the city can take place only after that final overthrow. From another point of view, however, the descent of the city, the conflict with the dragon, and the entry of the nations into the city, are all interlocking processes which together extend throughout the Christian dispensation. Something similar must be said with regard to the analogy between the present situation of the church militant and the transfiguration scene in the gospels. On both sides of the analogy the mystery of the Christ *as a whole* is mysteriously present in what is a part of that whole. As the transfiguration scene spans all revelation in its symbolism, so the church by virtue of her identity with Jesus in the one flesh is, in her present low estate, the earthen vessel which not only conveys the whole substance of the Christ-mystery, but is also mysteriously one with it in life, character and destiny.

V

The scriptural images suggest that in Christ a new provision has been made for human nature, but one which may be selfishly abused. In the continuing Christian conflict a safeguard against spiritual confusion will be found in the 'single eye' of a Christ-like 'simplicity'. By access to the mind of Christ the church is equipped with insight to appraise rightly the problems of human life.

How then do the peoples of the world make their entry into the city of God? That is a crucial question which opens up a further stage in this investigation. In our Lord's parable the birds find a resting-place under the shade of the mustard tree; in the seer's vision the nations walk in the city's light. The two images convey the same truth. The new order of the Christ pro-

---

[1] See above, § ii, pars. 1 and 2.

vides support and guidance for human life. The spiritual refreshment and illumination which issue forth from our Saviour in
and through the church are precisely the remedies which our
drooping strength and clouded vision need. In the new organism of Christ's body there is exhibited, at least in germinal form,
that re-integration of human life, for which, consciously or unconsciously, fallen man craves. In the new creation there begin
to appear once more the true outlines of the original creative
design; and thus a new framework is provided into which the
broken fragments of human life may be fitted. Moreover, the
mystery of the Christ, re-enacted in the church, is the new magnetic centre of attraction which draws all men unto itself. It is,
however, a fact that in the response to that magnetic drawing
there is more than one step to be taken; and to this the two
images of the mustard tree and the holy city may be thought to
bear witness.

The birds seek shade for themselves under the spreading
branches of the tree; the nations seek light from the city to guide
their steps. Our fallen nature comes to Christ to get what it can
for itself. The old Adam in all of us would like to turn the
resources of the new life to its own selfish uses. The shining city
of God is surrounded by a dark penumbra of folk, who, as in
Nehemiah's day, camp outside the walls for their own profit.[1]
These are people who do not desire to approach the sanctuary
within. For that would involve sacrifices which they are not prepared to make. They would prefer to enjoy the light which
proceeds from the sanctuary without themselves entering the
sanctuary. There are benefits which they would gladly enjoy, as
parasites, without being asked to give in return. In short, they
would like (as the saying is) to 'eat their cake and have it'. They
cannot truly enter the city without bringing with them their
'glory and honour', to be laid at the feet of the Lamb. To this
point, quite literally, *they cannot bring themselves*. So they linger at
the gates, evading the decisive issue. For the open gates of the
city constitute a challenge, not only to the powers of darkness,
but also to our fallen nature.

At this point we may recall what I have written previously
concerning the nature of the conflict in which we are engaged.[2]
It is like a wrestling match in which the combatants are the old

---

[1] Nehem. 13[16-21].   [2] See *Dominion*, Ch. V, § iii.

Adam and the New Man, a contest which goes on within each of us. The conflict, indeed, is joined between the church and the world. But since the old Adam is in all of us the 'world' is within the visible church as well as without. Moreover, beyond the boundaries of the visible church, and in spheres of life and thought where her authority is not recognized, the image of God still persists in this nature of ours, ever manifesting its presence in new and unexpected forms. Thus, in the close-locked embrace of the wrestlers it becomes wellnigh impossible at times to distinguish the two opposing sides. In the cloud of dust which gathers round the ever-changing aspects of the conflict we see not our tokens clearly. It is no wonder, then, if Christ our Lord appears at times under the repellant guise of the serpent, while Satan himself is transformed into an angel of light.[1]

In such specious guise the enemy of mankind ever seeks to corrupt that simplicity of faith which alone can keep the church faithful to her true Lord and spouse; so St Paul tells us in a passage which may thus be roughly summarized.[2] In that pronouncement of the apostle there is a key-word which I have rendered 'simplicity', but which can also mean 'liberality' or 'generosity'.[3] It is that quality of sincerity and directness which is a distinguishing mark in the noblest type of character. He who possesses this quality is able to see the best in other people precisely because his own character is rooted in humility. He has the 'single eye' of which our Lord spoke; so that with clear and direct glance he sees things in their true colours. For that very reason there is nothing sentimental about his simplicity. In seeing the good he is not blind to real faults of character. Such a person escapes the two opposite dangers of worldliness on the one hand and self-righteousness on the other. He thus evades two of the principal snares besetting the path of those who seek to live the good life. These same snares, however, also beset the path of the church in her mission to the world. Amongst the more grave disasters which could happen to any particular church would be the corruption of that very simplicity which is a principal safeguard.

This safeguarding quality which is so indispensable to the life of the church is derived from the Christ in whom alone it was

[1] 2 Cor. 11[14].   [2] 2 Cor. 11[2, 3].
[3] As it clearly does in 8[2] of this same epistle.

perfectly manifested. Christian simplicity is a partaking in the simplicity of the Christ. It is, in essence, that lowly faith and devotion to our Lord whereby we enter into and become identified with his devotion to the will of his Father. Thus the simplicity of the church is nothing else than a whole-hearted participation in the obedience of the Christ. Just so far, therefore, as the church is identified with her Lord in his single eye to God's glory, she will regard the problems of human life from his standpoint and will have a share in his penetrating insight into the enigma of human nature. That enigma, moreover, is a consequence of our fallen condition which has two aspects. On the one hand, as was pointed out in the preceding volume of this series,[1] Jesus discerned marks of the divine image in those who responded to his teaching. In such persons he saw the original design of creation, finding in them bonds of kinship with himself in whom that design was restored. On the other hand, as St John points out, he was under no illusions about men. He did not trust himself to them; for he knew what was in them.[2]

In our Lord's attitude to human nature there was no room for the smallest trace of sentimentalism. He knew that the promise of good in man could be brought to fulfilment only through a genuine response to his own challenging invitation: 'Take my yoke upon you and learn of me.' It is this insight into our humanity to which the church has access through partaking in the simplicity of the Christ; and it is through a share in such insight that the church is equipped to fulfil her proper function in the apostolic mission to the world. In that mission there is no room for worldly cynicism with its low estimate concerning the possibilities of good in man. On the other hand, it is also true that there is no place in that mission for the opposite error,—a romantic idealization of human nature which turns a blind eye to man's fallen state. Finally, the insight to which the church has access excludes the censorious attitude of self-righteousness which despises the day of small things, treating with harsh contempt those feeble signs and wavering gestures wherein the first humble beginnings of better things appear.

[1] *Dominion*, pp. 9–11 and 102.
[2] John 2[24, 25].

vi

The church identified with Jesus in a challenge to mankind in accordance with that divine method of evoking free response which safeguards human integrity. Fulfilment of the old in the new (Matt. 5[17, 18]), of creation in Christ and the church. Three aspects of the redemptive process: (1) Two parallel laws of life; (2) a ladder with two steps; (3) ascent of man into the descending city of God. To this threefold mystery the Transfiguration provides the master-key.

From what has just been said there follows an important conclusion. Just so far as the church, sharing her Lord's insight, becomes partaker in his obedience, to that extent her mission to the world will be conformed to the whole method of God's dealings with man in history. This method is manifested in the very form of the biblical revelation. God came down to the level of man and imparted the knowledge of himself by slow stages, as men were able to bear it. In that respect the condescending love embodied in the Incarnation was foreshadowed by the whole dispensation of the Old Testament. God respects the divine image which he himself has imprinted upon man. He will not violate that capacity for response which he himself has bestowed. His method is one which requires human co-operation at every stage. He is content to wait upon that degree of finite response which he can freely win from our frailty. He never forces the pace. His kingdom begins like the lowly mustard seed; yet it has a transforming-power which reaches out to embrace all things. Moreover, in those whom it embraces it promotes a likeness to itself, a simplicity of faith 'as a grain of mustard seed' to which, in the end, nothing is impossible.[1]

With this divine method our Lord wholly identified himself; and that fact is illustrated typically in the story of his temptations in the wilderness. All the suggestions of the tempter involved a winning of human allegiance at the price of human integrity; whereas the Lamb of God can justify 'the many' only by an appeal to their true nature,—that nature which corresponds precisely to what he himself is, inasmuch as he is the very mould in which they were originally created. Here we see the

---

[1] Matt. 17[20]; cp. Luke 17[6].

eternal challenge which is implicit in the simplicity of the Christ. Moreover, just so far as the church, through partaking in that simplicity, truly presents the challenge to mankind, the fulfilment of her mission will conform to the pattern seen by the seer of the Revelation. In the church so presenting her Master's challenge the lowly descent of the heavenly city will bring the Lamb of God down to the peoples, that he in turn may draw them up to himself.

Our Lord's tender regard for the integrity of our nature corresponds to his fulfilment of the prophecy concerning the elect Servant, of whom it was said that he does not break the bruised reed nor quench the smoking flax.[1] He does not annul the lesser good, because in a mixed world it is not yet as he would have it. So, instead of uprooting the tares for the sake of the wheat he lets both grow together until the harvest. This divine method does not condone the presence of evil; rather does it safeguard the integrity of the good. If the peoples are to bring their glory and honour to the sanctuary of the Lamb, they must do so freely. If they choose to linger at the gates of the city, or to sun themselves parasitically in its light outside the walls, they must have liberty so to do. They cannot be forced to enter; but also they must not be lured by flattery or by false promises which pander to their dislike of discipline. The descent of the holy city does not condone sin. Rather does it confront mankind with the wrath of the Lamb which is the complement and counterpart of his lowly meekness and of his sacrificial glory.

In St Matthew's report of the Sermon on the Mount our Lord prefaces the major part of his address with these words:

> Think not that I came to destroy the law or the prophets;
> I came not to destroy but to fulfil (Matthew 5[17]).

The context of this saying indicates its application. Our Lord did not, by his coming, abrogate the moral law of the old covenant. On the contrary, notwithstanding the fact that its imperfections conflict with his own perfect law of love, he yet declares that it shall continue in its integrity 'until all things be accomplished'.[2] This mysterious saying looks in two directions. In one sense all things were accomplished when the law and the prophets were fulfilled in the sacrifice of Christ. In *that* sense the

---

[1] Matt. 12[20], citing Isa. 42[3].   [2] Matt. 5[18].

substance of 'the law' has passed away—not, however, by destruction, but by fulfilment. It has been transformed in Christ without loss of validity, as humanity has been transformed in him without loss of integrity. That double truth was indicated as regards both its parts in the mystery of our Lord's transfiguration. What is fulfilled in Christ is not destroyed; for death is not the end of sacrifice. What is fulfilled in Christ passes into a new form, unlike its old form; it is transfigured *in* its fulfilment. Thus the lowly form of the old covenant was taken up by transformation into the more glorious form of the new covenant, as the insignificant mustard seed is changed into the spreading mustard-tree.

So the mysterious saying has a second meaning. The two creations overlap in Christendom. The visible church belongs to the second creation, but must live in the first creation as an outpost of the heavenly city. The church militant is like an army serving in a foreign land. Or, varying the military metaphor, we may say that the camp of the new Israel must continue its movement through the wilderness of this fallen world until the last enemy is destroyed and the pilgrimage ends in the New Jerusalem. In *that* sense all things still await their accomplishment. The marks of the divine image in man, however fragmentary, are not superseded by the new creation; for the purpose embodied in the new is the restoration of the old, not its annulment. The healing process of the new creation is ever at work upon the old order, tending towards the restoration of its original harmony. When this process is completed the old will have been wholly resolved into the new. Until then the old order retains its validity; the fragmentary and relative good remains alongside the best. In traditional western terminology, the Natural Law continues alongside the Law of Christ.

This statement, however, is only a partial representation of the truth. The relationship between the two creations is actually more mysterious. They lie 'alongside' each other in this present dispensation only in the sense that, closely connected and co-related as they are in human life, they yet remain always distinct, and, further, have equal validity and importance. This must be so; for both are indispensable, since neither suffices without the other. The second creation, presupposing the first, is unintelligible without it; whereas the first requires the second for its own redemption and fulfilment. These considerations suggest, however, that the relationship between the two creations might be more exactly represented by the picture of a ladder which has two steps, the first leading up to the second. But if this conception is to be adequate to the facts we shall have to say that the first step has sunk below the position which it occupied in the original plan of creation.[1] It is, therefore, only by ascending into the new creation that men can rise to the level for which God originally predestined them. The peoples of the world must 'go up' from the earthly city to the city of God, as Israel of old went up to Jerusalem.[2]

But thirdly, the picture of the ladder with two steps still leaves the two creations 'alongside' one another in the sense that there is no radical correlation between them. Moreover, the ascent from the first step to the second implies that the first step has been left behind. That implication, however, does not do justice to the vision in the Revelation. For there the glory and honour of the first creation are brought into the second. This, again, is brought about through the fact that the second creation descends to earth. The nations go up into the city, because the city comes down to them. These three ways of envisaging the relationship between the two creations, namely (i) the two parallel laws, (ii) the ladder with two steps, and (iii) the ascent of mankind into the descending city, are all necessary to the full truth of the mystery. But finally, justice can be done to all three aspects of the truth only if the mystery is interpreted in the light of our Lord's transfiguration. For there the perfect humanity was transfigured by the divine glory which surrounded it. The glory thus surrounding the flesh of Jesus symbolized the return of creation to its Creator through the embrace of man by the condescending love of God.

The flesh of Jesus was so transfigured, because, as the beloved Son of the Father, he had himself embraced 'all flesh' when he accepted the lowly form and destiny of the Servant in whom the scriptures are fulfilled. So the first creation is transfigured in the second creation just so far as by entry into the second the first receives the form of the Servant who is the Lamb of God. So

---

[1] The sunken step would then represent 'the relative natural law' in fallen humanity.

[2] cp. Isa. 2[1, 2].

51

long as this process remains incomplete the two creations remain distinct, and there is ascent from one to the other. Yet the two are one in the flesh of the Lamb; and he himself is that sanctuary of the descending city in which creation is embraced by the Creator.[1] Just so far as the process of transfiguration is effected, the glory and honour of the first creation attain their true end in God. The treasures of human nature, and therefore also the treasures of *all* nature return to the design of God's original plan as it is fulfilled in Christ. Since, however, the transfiguration in the mortal flesh of Jesus only *foreshadowed* the final glory of his resurrection, so too the process which we are now considering can only foreshadow the final manifestation of God's city. This happens through the medium of the visible church, but in such wise that the foregleams of the New Jerusalem proleptically bathe the whole of the first creation in their transfiguring rays. For the transfigured flesh of Jesus was the 'all flesh' of creation which he had taken to himself.

[1] See Rev. 21[22, 23]. The Shekinah glory of the divine presence becomes manifested as it is refracted through the glorified humanity of the Lamb.

CHAPTER III

VOCATION AND WORSHIP

i

The divine invitation to a wedding-feast is mediated through a bride prepared, whose 'adornment' is the 'order' of the new creation. The call of God is creative, and has cosmic significance. The scriptural parallel between creation by the Word and the call of God's people implies in both creations an ordered harmony of individual functions. The Creator answered sin's discords by a creative call of Israel the Servant out of sinful non-existence into a cosmic drama of harmonious co-operation.

The New Jerusalem descending from heaven to earth constitutes a challenge to the peoples, summoning them to enter her open gates. But further, the city descends 'prepared as a bride adorned for her husband'.[1] The summons, therefore, is that gracious invitation of which our Lord spoke in his parable of the wedding-feast which a king made for his son.[2] For 'blessed are they who are called to the marriage-supper of the Lamb'.[3] He who accepts the invitation, however, must—like the bride herself—be adorned for the feast. He must enter the banquet-chamber arrayed in a wedding-garment.[4] He must be clothed in the righteousness of Christ. Thus, the invitation to the feast, like the summons to enter the city, is a challenge to all men to 'put on' the obedience of the Christ,[5]—a call to gird themselves with that humility which Jesus displayed when he girded himself with a towel to wash the disciples' feet.[6] It is clear, then, that in the Christian dispensation the invitation to the feast and the summons to enter the city are, in fact, one and the same thing. It would agree perfectly with the symbolism of scripture if we said that men receive the summons to the bridal festivities through the new Eve, the partner of Christ's obedience.[7]

[1] Rev. 21[2].   [2] Matt. 22[1-14]; cp. Luke 14[15-24].   [3] See Rev. 19[7-9].
[4] Matt. 22[11, 12].   [5] Gal. 3[27], Eph. 4[24].   [6] 1 Pet. 5[5], John 13[4 ff].
[7] See above, Ch. I, §§ iii ff. The complex image of the city-bride starts from Gen. 2[22], where Eve is 'built' (cp. RV margin ad loc.).

The voice of the bridegroom is heard through the bride as a composer is heard through singers' voices or through musical instruments. The message of Jesus to mankind is embodied in his church. We may perhaps venture to add that only so far as the church is prepared as a bride 'adorned' for her husband will men rightly apprehend the 'order' of the new creation. This thought might well have been in the seer's mind. For the same Greek word (*kosmos*) means both 'order' and 'adornment'. Amidst the disorder of a fallen world the order of the new creation is manifested in the beauty and harmony of design with which the 'very varied' wisdom of God is even now clothing redeemed humanity.[1] It is in this way that the descending city constitutes the invitation. Just so far as the obedience of the Christ is exhibited in the church the call of God sounds clearly so that all may hear. The summons to the wedding-feast, however, has a wider background in scripture which connects it with the creative activity of God. In the Book of Proverbs the invitation is issued by the divine Wisdom who is the beginning of God's ways in creation; and the feast is prepared in the house which Wisdom has built.[2] The fruits of God's love can be enjoyed by man only within that order which the Creator himself has designed and framed.

But further, the call of God is itself a creative act of the divine Word. In the scriptural idiom God creates by calling things or persons out of non-existence into existence. The 'God said' of Genesis 1 is variously echoed throughout both the testaments. A typical passage is Psalm 33[6-9]. But for our present purpose Isaiah 48[12, 13] is especially relevant. In verse 12 Israel is referred to by the deity as 'my called one'; and in the next verse the creation of heaven and earth is referred to with a repetition of the same word: 'When I call them they stand together.' Heaven and earth 'stand up' in response to the divine call;[3] they 'stand forth' or 'appear', that is 'come into being', according to the dictionary.[4] This language is repeated by later Jewish writers,[5]

---

[1] This is one possible application of the untranslatable word in Eph. 3[10].

[2] Prov. 8[22]–9[6]; cp. 1[20-23] and 8[1-10]. See also Isa. 55, where the call to the messianic feast is followed by a 'new creation' scene effected by the Word of God.

[3] So RV.

[4] BDB, p. 764, col. 2.

[5] For which see *Revelation*, p. 232, note 2.

and is employed by St Paul in Romans 4^{17}, where God is referred
to as 'calling the things that are not as though they were', that
is to say: summoning them out of non-existence into existence.
In 1 Corinthians 1$^{26-28}$, however, we have a striking commentary upon the connexion between the two verses cited above
from Isaiah 48. Israel is 'my called one' in a sense to which
the creative 'calling' of heaven and earth into existence by the
Creator is conceived to be parallel. The call is creative in both
instances; and in both the call evokes a capacity for response.[1]
So, when the apostle invites the Christians at Corinth to 'consider your calling, brethren', he links their election into the new
creation with a choosing by the Creator of 'the things that are
not' (verse 28).

We must now take note of the fact that things thus created by
the divine voice are called, not only into existence, but also into
a particular form of existence corresponding to the function
alloted to them in the divine plan of creation. For they are not
only called to their places in the order of creation. They are
also called by their names, thus receiving their distinctive
identity.[2] Moreover, they answer the divine roll-call, standing
up together and saying: 'Lo! here we are.'[3] In this way the
word of God creates a *kosmos* in which all things have their
appropriate places. So in John 1$^{4-10}$ *kosmos* is the created product of *Logos*. The Johannine use of *kosmos* may have been suggested by the fact that in the Septuagint the Book of Genesis is
called *Genesis kosmou* (the beginning of the world-order). The
same Greek word recurs in Isaiah 40^{26}, where the Hebrew reference to the stars as 'their host' is replaced by the expression:
'his *kosmos*.' The host of the stars is God's 'order', an 'adornment' of bright jewels with which he has decked his creation.
Here again a parallel recurs between the heavenly lights and the
elect of a new creation who shall 'shine as the stars for ever and
ever'.[4] Creation was thus designed to be like an orchestral or
dramatic performance in which every created object plays the

[1] For other implications of the parallel see *Revelation*, p. 239 with notes.

[2] Gen. 1$^{3-10}$, Isa. 40^{26}, Ps. 147^4. The naming of the animals by Adam in
Gen. 2 completes the naming in Gen. 1, and brings out the implication that
a name confers specific identity.

[3] Judith 9^6 interpreting Isa. 48^{13}.

[4] Dan. 12^3; cp. Matt. 13^{43}, and Phil. 2^{15} (as rendered by Moffatt): 'Ye
shine like stars in a dark world.'

precise part to which it has been summoned by the divine conductor or producer.[1]

When this harmonious design was marred by the discords of sin the Creator summoned into existence his chosen people and called Israel out of Egypt (Hosea 11[1]), making the summons effective by his creative acts of power. Thus the vocation of Israel as God's Servant became inseparably connected in scripture with the doctrine of creation, and eventually with the expectation of a new creation. This conjunction of ideas is a constant feature of the second Isaiah. As once God called Israel from Egypt, so now once more from Babylon, making good the summons, as of old, by fresh acts of creative power. Moreover, as nature is invoked to assist the chosen people once more, so too the Gentile king, Cyrus, is enrolled as an anointed saviour of Israel whose path will be smoothed by the Creator. In all this the *call* of Israel and the *creation* of Israel as God's Servant seem to have become practically synonymous terms. The call is described in creationist language, as in 44[1-3] and in 49[1, 5].[2] Moreover, as Ezekiel learnt, the return of Israel from captivity was to be a creative act of God like a summons of dead men from their graves to a new and risen life.[3] Characteristic Pauline statements already quoted above show that these ideas are also dominant in the New Testament. The call of the new Israel is regarded as a summons from the non-existence of the old life to a new existence in Christ.

ii

The creative call in the gospel story. New creation as resurrection from the dead (Ezekiel 37, Romans 4, John 5 and 11). In Johannine teaching this theme reaches from the first creation to the last things. The parallel between Isaiah 40 and John 10 (stars and sheep called by name). The completeness and unity of the created order reproduced in the flock of Christ. Individual vocation fulfilled within an ordered whole which embraces all individual responses.

It can now be affirmed that when Jesus called men to follow him this was a summons to enter the new creation; the call itself

[1] Some such imagery is suggested by Ps. 19 and by Job 38[7].
[2] For the former passage see my *Confirmation*, p. 131.   [3] Ezek. 37.

was a typically creative act, one of a series by which the new Israel was formed. It was a summons to enter into partnership with the Christ in the mission of the Servant by which Adam's dominion is restored. Further, we have noticed that the typically creative act of Israel's restoration was envisaged by the prophet Ezekiel under the figure of a resurrection from the dead. This way of speaking continues in the New Testament. In the argument of Romans 4[17-25] the apostle first describes the deity as he who quickens the dead and creatively calls non-existent things into existence. He then proceeds to speak of Isaac's birth from aged parents as a bringing forth of life from the dead, thus foreshadowing the resurrection of the Christ.[1] In St John's Gospel this theme has also a prominent place. In Chapter 5 we find identically the same expression for 'quickening the dead' as in Romans 4[17]. Moreover, its connexion with the creative call is here more fully elaborated. For the discourse in which that connexion occurs follows immediately upon a typical sabbath healing. This Jesus justifies by referring to the continuous working which occupies the sabbath-rest of the Creator (5[17]).

The parallel between the Father and the Son concerning creative 'working' in verse 17 is continued in the statements concerning 'quickening the dead' (verses 21 *ff*). What follows makes it clear that the dead are quickened by the creative call of the Son of God, about which two things may be said. First, the language employed illustrates the teaching of the prologue. God creates by his Word; and in the new creation this takes place through the voice of the Word incarnate. Secondly, the quickening of the dead by the Son belongs to the present as well as to the final summons at the last day. As elsewhere in the apostolic writings, the Last Things have their inception in the gospel history. This was to receive classic exemplification in the raising of Lazarus; but there, as here, the language employed suggests that the incarnate Lord by his creative summons raises the spiritually dead to new life in that new order which he is even now inaugurating. The phrase concerning 'hearing my word and believing' (5[24]) indicates a passage 'from death to life' which can be illustrated from the story of the man born blind in Chapter 9. The relation of that incident to creation on

[1] And repeating a typical piece of prophetic imagery, for which see *Dominion*, Ch. V, §§ iv, v.

the one hand and to resurrection on the other has been explained by me elsewhere.[1]

The creative call of God in Christ not only makes men new creatures, but also, as in the first creation, summons them by name.[2] This is particularly noticeable in St John's Gospel where Lazarus is summoned by name from the tomb and Mary is called by name from the griefs of the tomb to the joys of the new life.[3] These are examples which illustrate the allegory of the Good Shepherd. For 'the sheep hear his voice, and *he calleth his own sheep by name* and *leadeth them out* (John 10[3]). The language here used has an exact verbal parallel in Isaiah 40[26], with, however, one remarkable difference. The prophetic passage refers not to sheep but to stars:

> Lift up your eyes and see who created these,
> Who *leadeth out* their host by number;
> *He calls to them all by name.*
> By the greatness of his might, and for that
>   he is strong in power
> Not one is lacking.

The identity of language can scarcely be accidental. For the fourth evangelist shows a special interest in the Book of Isaiah and particularly in the 'servant' prophecies which begin with this chapter. Moreover, in Isaiah 40 the Creator who leads out the stars is also the divine Shepherd who leads out his flock from Babylon. The arm which guides the stars is also the arm which carries the lambs and gently leads the ewes (verses 10, 11).

Now in the section of this prophecy which connects the flock of Israel with the starry heavens there is a magnificent description of the divine omnipotence in creation. The inference intended is clear. As not one star is lacking from the sky, so not one sheep will be lacking from the flock. The two creations are united in their Creator; his will is manifested in the second as in the first. The same law runs through both. So we may safely

---

[1] See *Revelation*, Ch. VI, § iv (2), pp. 177–182. It is, perhaps, not wholly accidental that both Chs. 5 and 11 in St John are followed by a banquet story (Chs. 6 and 12[1-8]) which may be held to typify the bridal-feast of the new creation (12[1], 'six days').

[2] cp. above, § i, par. 4.

[3] 11[43, 44], 20[16]. For the Johannine emphasis upon names see also 1[6], 1[40-45], 11[1-5], 12[1-4], 21[15-17]. For a synoptic parallel we have Matt. 16 (Bar-Jonah, Peter) on which see *Dominion*, Ch. VI, § iii.

argue from one to the other. The Creator's power does not fail, nor his purpose fall short of achievement. Accordingly, as his sovereign authority is manifested and vindicated in the stability and order of the first creation, so must it be also in the second. In the analogy one point, in particular, stands out. As the stars are summoned by name to their places in the drama of the heavenly *kosmos*, so the Good Shepherd summons the sheep by name as he leads out the flock. The completeness of the created order is due to the twofold fact that no detail is overlooked by the wisdom of God and that nothing is wanting in the translation of the design into effect. But so also is it with the flock of the Good Shepherd. 'His own' sheep are known to him individually, and not one of them shall perish; for none shall pluck them out of his hand. The ground of this confident assertion is then disclosed. What is in the Shepherd's hand is in the Father's hand; for they two are one (John 10²⁷⁻³⁰).¹

The *completeness* of the chosen flock is a matter of tender concern in St John's Gospel; and its *unity* is frequently emphasized.² The two ideas are complementary; and together they suggest that the elect, in their total number, form the constituent elements of a *kosmos*, wherein the unity and completeness of the original *kosmos* are to be restored.³ That is one aspect of a very familiar passage which might be paraphrased as follows: 'So greatly did God love the order which he had created that he gave his only Son for its salvation; and this ultimate goal is to be reached through the attainment of eternal life by every believer in the Son' (John 3¹⁵⁻¹⁷).⁴ Not one shall be lacking; that is the law of both creations, as it is also manifested in the completeness of divine judgement (Isaiah 34¹⁶). But the full tale of the flock, as of the created order, is important for a double reason: (1) The individual is called 'by name' to fulfil a particular function; and it is precisely for this that he was called into existence. His con-

---

¹ In Isa. 40¹² the Creator-Shepherd measures the waters in the hollow of his hand, and the heavens with the span of his hand. Perhaps we may see here further evidence of a literary connexion with John 10. The scriptural emphasis upon the hands of God received more precise dogmatic form in the second century, for which see *Revelation*, pp. 169–172.

² cp. 6³⁷⁻⁴⁰, 11⁵², 17¹²*ff*, and the alternative text of 10²⁹ (RV margin).

³ cp. above § i, par. 4 on the LXX use.

⁴ With the twice repeated πᾶς here cp. the repetition of πᾶν and πᾶς in John 6³⁷⁻⁴⁵.

tribution is needed to make up the harmony of the whole. For no voice shall be missing in the celestial choir. Yet (2) it is the individual who must answer the call. The sheep must hear the shepherd's voice and respond to it. Every performer, orchestral or dramatic, must co-operate with the leader. If one fails, the planned whole is incomplete; the result does not correspond with the author's design. On the one hand vocation is not merely individual; it finds its significance in the ordered whole which the Creator planned. On the other hand this ordered whole is precisely the unity of *all* responses. Hence the deep concern of the Shepherd for the one sheep missing, and the joy of the heavenly choir over its restoration.[1] Not one must be lacking.

iii

In both creations the Creator-Shepherd 'counts' his flock by name. Under both 'covenants' of creation there is unbroken continuity of form as well as completeness. The messianic community is an ordered mystery of unity embracing plurality with organic ministerial sequence. Jesus, as head of the new creation, responds to the Father's call, and includes us in his vocation as sharers in his new name. Human vocation is truly significant only in the Christ.

The Johannine revelation that the all-prevailing power of divine love is present in the protective care of the Good Shepherd is expressed by means of a Hebrew idiom concerning 'the hand' ($10^{28, 29}$) which suggests a whole train of biblical associations.[2] In the promised restoration of Israel which Jeremiah records it is said that in the holy land 'shall the flocks again pass along under the hands of him that *telleth* them'.[3] Here the shepherd's hand counts the sheep as they pass to make sure that none is missing. The same Hebrew word for 'counting' is used in Psalm 147^4, where we read: 'He *telleth* the number of the stars'; and there follows the striking phrase: 'To them all he calls names.' Once more the passage in Isaiah 40 provides the key. The Creator is likened to a shepherd numbering his flock. As the stars in their courses move under his 'hand' he calls out their

---

[1] Luke 15^{3-7}.
[2] See also above, § ii, last par. but one, final note.   [3] Jer. 33^{13}.

names to them all.[1] But further, in Jeremiah 33 this theme receives an important development. The picture of the shepherd counting his flock suggests another aspect of the 'completeness' which is conspicuous in all these passages. Not one sheep is missing in the restored Israel. But also, not one shepherd is missing either! David shall never want a man to sit upon the throne; and the temple shall never want a priest to offer sacrifice.[2]

Finally the analogy between the two creations is affirmed in its most explicit form:

> If ye can break my covenant of the day and my covenant of the
>   night, . . .
> Then may also my covenant be broken with David my servant . . .
> and with the Levites, the priests, my ministers.
> As the host of heaven cannot be numbered, neither the sand of the
>   sea measured;
> So will I multiply the seed of David my servant,
> and the Levites that minister unto me (Jeremiah 33[19-22]).

In the conclusion the seed of David is traced back to its source in the seed of Abraham, to whom a like promise had been made: 'He led him forth abroad and said . . . Count the stars, if thou be able to count them; . . . so shall thy seed be' (Genesis 15[5]). In these statements the total numbers in both orders are beyond human counting; yet all the details of both are comprehended by the deity. Behind the creative call in both spheres lie all the resources of divine wisdom and power. The foreshadowed messianic community, therefore, is a cosmic mystery[3] which trans-

---

[1] Wisd. 11[24, 25] (i) declares the Creator's love for 'all the things that are' without exception, and (ii) traces the continuance and preservation of every created thing to the divine will as expressed in the creative call. The phraseology of this passage has some close parallels in NT, e.g. Rom. 4[17], John 15[9, 10], 17[11, 12].

[2] Jer. 33[14-18]. David's tree (the stock of Jesse in Isa. 11[1], the royal vine in Ezek. 19[10-14]) is completed in the messianic 'Branch' (Jer. 33[14-16]). The double promise of this passage finds an echo in 2 Chron. 13[10-12]; but it found its fulfilment in Christ and the apostles. Cp. my essay in *The Apostolic Ministry*.

[3] This is strongly suggested by the figure of the new Eve in Rev. 12[1 ff]. The twelve stars which crown her head correspond to the twelve tribes as seen in Joseph's dream (Gen. 37[9]). cp. Rev. 7[4-8]; and contrast the cosmic confusion symbolized by the dragon's action in 12[4]. On this see further below, Ch. IV.

cends human understanding. Yet, on the other hand, it is a unity so designed that all its parts have a necessary place in the plan of the whole, as that whole is perfectly known to God. In these two complementary aspects of its completeness the second creation corresponds to the first. But thirdly the messianic community is complete in the perpetuity of its royal headship and in the continuity of its ministerial succession, a promise which is fulfilled in the Holy Catholic Church.

We have just now seen the continuity of Israel's call traced back through David to Abraham, and forward without a break to its messianic culmination.[1] Ezekiel's discourse on the flock of Israel closes with a corresponding picture of the messianic age which concludes as follows: 'Ye my sheep, the sheep of my pasture, are men and I am your God' (Ezekiel 34[31]). This might mean no more than that under the image of a shepherd and his sheep God's care for man is depicted (cp. 34[12ff]). The explanation, however, is actually superfluous unless we give it the double meaning of the Hebrew original. For the English word 'men' here renders the Hebrew word 'Adam' which is both a generic term and also an individual name. Now if the flock of Israel is thus identified with Adam we get excellent sense. The messianic future has just been described in 'new creation' terms. The holy land is to become the new pasture of an earthly paradise into which the divine Shepherd will lead his flock by the hand of his servant David. In this new beginning the flock of Israel is restored to the function of Adam, the human head of creation. Here the continuity is traced forward through the kingdom of David to the community of the new Adam.

Under the new covenant all the types are united in Jesus. He is the divine Shepherd who, like Joshua, yet as the promised king of David's line, leads his people out of the wilderness into the pastures of the messianic kingdom. He does so, however, as the new head of creation. Adam called all the creatures by their names; and Jesus calls all his sheep by name. But in calling them the second Adam recreates them in himself. The paradise regained into which he leads them is his Body, where they become 'one flesh' with him. Thus the divine voice in Ezekiel, by attaching the name of Adam to 'the sheep of my pasture', foreshadowed the truth that Jesus imprints his own 'new name' upon all who

_____
[1] Jer. 33[14-26].

become new creatures in him.[1] The creative call of God in the new creation is the call heard and answered by the One New Man, the Servant of the Lord. By his response to the call of the Father, however, he also made that call accessible to us, and opened our ears to hear it. Thus he won the right to include us in his vocation, the many in the One. This he does as the Creator-Word incarnate by calling us into union with himself, that we may participate in his obedience. Moreover, only through such participation is it possible for each of us to fulfil his true vocation. In this respect the visible church is the effectual sign of human destiny. Only through unity of vocation with Christ and in Christ can mankind become a society where vocation has abiding significance.

iv

In NT the divine Shepherd becomes the Lamb whose self-oblation constitutes a creative call of leadership to 'the many'. In Revelation (i) the Davidic type is fulfilled in the victorious Lamb and his sacrificial following (Chs. 5, 14); of this (ii) the three-fold name upon the disciple (3^{12}) shows the personal implications, which (iii), as a part in the whole, attain actuality in the redeemed community. God is to be vindicated in his Servant (Jesus and his church) through the response of 'the many' in the One.

The unity of all vocations in the one vocation of the Christ makes possible the harmony of all responses in his one response to the Father; and this unity of vocation and response in Jesus is the essential pattern of that *kosmos* which is the new creation. The many are called into the One, that the diversities of creation may once more become a manifold unity in that One. Moreover, the significance of the new unity is precisely the significance of the One in whom it exists. This doctrine is implicit in the New Testament as a whole, and becomes explicit particularly in Johannine and Pauline forms. In St John's Gospel the Shepherd 'goes before' the sheep and they 'follow him, for they know his voice'. Jesus went before them on the journey which led to Calvary and beyond.[2] In laying down his

[1] See above, Ch. I, § v, last two pars., but one, with note.
[2] cp. John 10^4 with $14^{2,\ 12,\ 28}$. In all these passages 'go' represents the same Greek word.

life the Shepherd was revealed to be the Lamb of God.[1] For this reason 'the many' recognize in him the true Servant of the Lord, so that they are drawn to follow him along his path of sacrifice. The 'drawing' of the Father through the passion of the uplifted Servant constitutes a creative call by which 'the many' are both illuminated and united.[2] In their witness to the fulfilment of prophecy the two 'Johannine' books, the gospel and the apocalypse, both teach that the divine Shepherd of Isaiah 40^{11} became the lamb that was led to the slaughter in Isaiah 53^7; and Revelation 7^{17} attributes the divine functions of Isaiah $49^{9, 10}$ to the Servant lamb of 53^7. In the Revelation, however, it is as *the victorious Lamb* that Jesus fulfils the shepherd's function of leadership. For his sacrificial self-oblation to the Father is the way by which as 'one flock' the redeemed enter the peace and harmony of the new order.[3]

In Revelation $5^{5, 6}$ 'the lamb that was slain' is described as 'the lion of the tribe of Judah, the root of David'; and in the scene which follows victorious and universal sovereignty is ascribed to him on the ground of his redeeming sacrifice. In Chapter 14 the Davidic *motif* is renewed in a like paradoxical fashion. The lamb stands upon Mount Zion, as David did when he had conquered the Jebusite stronghold (2 Samuel 5); and, whereas in the next chapter David, fulfilling the traditional function of the ancient priest-king, offers a burnt offering before the ark of God, in the new order the type gives way to its fulfilment. The sovereignty of the lamb is constituted by his wholly sacrificial character. The identification of the messianic king with the Servant, suggested in the Septuagint version of Isaiah $53^{2,}$[4] is now complete, and a corresponding change appears in the retinue of the victorious lamb. Instead of the warrior host who had just subdued the Jebusites in David's story, the Lamb of God is surrounded by a new Israel who are described in language which suggests ceremonial purity. Their virginal status is that of he-lambs without blemish, fitted to be sacrificial victims of the cultus. They are conformed to the

---

[1] cp. John 10^{11-18} with 1^{29} and 19^{30-37}.

[2] John $6^{44, 45}$, 10^{16}, 12^{32}.

[3] Here we seem to approach the profound identity of thought which underlies the stark literary contrasts of the Revelation and the Gospel.

[4] See *Dominion*, pp. 83, 84.

sacrificial character of their victorious leader, as their title of 'first-fruits' indicates.[1] The manner in which this takes place must now be considered.

In Revelation 3[12] the risen Christ makes a threefold promise to the disciple who shares his triumph: 'I will write upon him the name of my God and the name of the city of my God, the New Jerusalem, which cometh down out of heaven from my God, and my own new name.' The disciple who is thus honoured has been built into the new sanctuary as a supporting pillar, and is, therefore, identified with its worship. Accordingly, he exhibits the essential characteristics alike of the new creation and of its Creator, which two are for ever united and identified in the sacrificial royalty of the Servant-Lamb. Yet in thus conferring the divine name in threefold form[2] upon those who share his victory Jesus does not impose upon them uniformity of type. For in the preceding chapter (2[17]) he promises to the victorious disciple 'a new name which no one knoweth save he who receiveth it'. The reference here would seem to be to the new character conferred upon each disciple; for 'name' stands for 'character' so frequently in scripture. There is, however, another possibility which cannot be excluded, namely, the revelation of God as apprehended differently by each disciple. But these two suggestions may easily be combined. The divine Name, that is the divinely given revelation of all that God is, is differently manifested in each disciple, according as each responds faithfully to his vocation, and what this signifies to each individual is his own peculiar secret.

Yet the manifestation which has this inalienably personal character is also related to the wider whole to which it properly belongs. For the name of God is made manifest to the world in and through the people of God; the glory of God is made accessible to mankind in the descending city. Moreover, the city of God derives its whole character from the Lamb in whom the name of God is perfectly manifested. Accordingly, every enrolled citizen of the New Jerusalem is, in his own measure, a

---

[1] Rev. 14[4, 5]; cp. Lev. 1[10] *et al.* In John 18[1] *ff* we have a corresponding paradox of divine supremacy in One who is about to be led as a lamb to the slaughter; for which see *The Apostolic Ministry*, p. 97, note 2.

[2] In this trinitarian presentation the Spirit is represented by the Bride. Cp. 22[17] and 21[2].

bearer of this threefold manifestation. As he responds to his vocation by participation in the obedience of the Christ, there is refracted in him one particular ray of the divine glory. His individual character in its uniqueness is the result of his personal response in his whole being to the light given to him. He is called 'by name' precisely that he may make this contribution. He does so, however, as a citizen of the heavenly city. His vocation is not fulfilled *in vacuo*. For only so far as it becomes a genuine function of the redeemed community does the individual's response to the divine call participate in the one response of the Christ. The divine glory is refracted in its fulness only in the luminary of the descending city, that is to say, in the *whole* city as bearer of the Lamb.

The promise of the new name is made to one who shall be 'a pillar in the temple of my God'. For, as we have seen, the place of transfiguration is also the place of worship so that in God's city the glory of the Shekinah and the flame of the burnt-offering are one.[1] In so far as the obedience of the Christ is being manifested to mankind *through* the church, this is because that obedience is being truly set forth before the Father *in* the church. For the church is the effectual sign of man's true destiny in Christ. The nations will come to acknowledge God in his Servant only through contemplating the Servant's sacrifice. Now the Servant is the whole Christ, that is, Jesus and his church. Accordingly the justification of the many nations *by* the Servant will come to pass through the justification of the many individuals *in* the Servant. The truth of this statement, however, depends upon the fact that in Scripture justification means vastly more than individual forgiveness. The truth of God is to be vindicated among the nations through the return of 'Israel' to her true vocation. This return takes place in the Christ, and is effected in the responses which all his members make to the creative call of Jesus in his Body.

V

Christ, the Church and the Christian. In the body completeness, including diversity of functions, involves equal necessity of all members with like honour for all. To this corresponds the social

[1] See above. Ch. I, § ii, last par. and note, with § vii; also Ch. II, § iii, par. 1.

harmony designed by the Creator and restored in Christ. The structure of the new creation received its form from the sacrifice of Jesus the Servant; and we are called to participate with him in the new unity of a worshipful life by identification with his self-oblation. This is the clue to 1 Corinthians 12–14.

The statements in the Revelation of St John concerning the relation of the individual disciple to the divine name and to the new name illustrate the fact that the new creation has a triadic form. This also appears from the following considerations: (*a*) The whole Christ is the One in the many, the Lamb in the city, Christ in the church, or conversely,—the many in the One, the members in the body. (*b*) This duality of the One Man, however, can also be expressed in another series: the Bridegroom and the bride, the Head and the body, the Messiah and the *ecclesia*. When we put the two types of statement together they are seen to yield three terms: Christ, the Church, and the individual Christian; and this threefold relationship is essential to the Christian conception of vocation both in its religious and in its social significance. The three terms here mentioned must not be confused with the threefoldness of the divine name in Revelation 3^{12}, although of course there is an intimate connexion between the two triads, as also between the two forms of the 'new name' (2^{17}, 3^{12}). For the fuller understanding of the threefold relationship (Christ, the church and the individual Christian) we turn next to the Pauline teaching concerning the body of Christ.

Here two points stand out: (1) The analogy between a community and a biological organism emphasizes the variety of functions exercised by the many members of the community. The unity is exhibited, not in uniformity, but in diversity; and this diversity of functions within a larger whole gives to the unity of that larger whole its deep significance. (2) The many members which are so diverse in function are all equally necessary to the full unity and significance of the whole. The body can exist without one or more of its members; yet in a mutilated state it is no longer a complete body. The second characteristic is inseparable from the first. Because each member fulfils a different function, and because each of the functions is necessary to the full life of the body, therefore all the members are equally

67

necessary to the life of the organism *in its completeness*. The last three words are crucial to the analogy developed in 1 Corinthians 12[12-27]. It is not here maintained that all the members are equally necessary for the body's *welfare*. That is a matter for further consideration. Fundamentally the Pauline doctrine of the 'mystical body' emphasizes the idea of completeness in manifoldness ('not one is lacking') which we have found to be so deeply rooted in the biblical analogy between the two creations.

The 'body' doctrine is indeed one of the modes of representation through which that analogy is carried over from the Old Testament to the New. This particular form of the analogy, however, emphasizes points of importance which, perhaps, could not be represented so adequately through any alternative. figure of speech. One of these points is brought out by St Paul when he declares that the principle of equal necessity among the members of the body carries with it a corollary of equal honour.[1] In saying this he implies that, unless such a corollary receives full recognition in the church, the significant unity of Christ's body will not be manifested. In the biological organism 'nature' shows equal care for all the parts in the sense that in a healthy body there is adequate provision for every part to fulfil its function in accordance with the needs of the whole. The striking differences which seem to us to make one organ more important or potent or significant in no way conflict with the dominance of this principle. For the principle is itself a manifestation of that form of unity which is fundamental to the living organism. In all this, moreover, the design of the Creator is clear. The welfare of the body depends upon the possibility of each part developing fully its special contribution to the whole.

This principle clearly holds good also for the social organism. No society can develop its full resources unless every member has scope to make his full contribution. On the other hand, in our fallen state sins of vainglory, self-seeking and cupidity continually undermine all efforts to attain this desirable end. Individual vocation is thus thwarted and the plan of creation is frustrated. Finally, this disorder is present also in the visible church, because the leaven of the old Adam is still at work within the members of Christ. Nevertheless the design of the

[1] 1 Cor. 12[21-26].

Creator has been restored through the obedience of the Christ; for the organism of the new creation received its distinctive form from the sacrifice of Calvary. The permanent temple of that sacrifice was built by Wisdom incarnate (the beginning of God's new ways)[1] when 'the Lord of the glory' was crucified. For the many died in the death of the One, and were called out of the nothingness of death into the new life of the one who died and rose again.[2] Christian vocation, therefore, being a summons to share in the one vocation of Jesus the Servant, is a call to participate, each according to the measure of the gift of the Christ,[3] in the new unity created by his sacrifice. This unity, moreover, is a unity of worship; and the substance of that worship to which we are called is precisely the sacrifice of God's true Servant, that is the obedience of the Christ.

It follows from this that the response of each to his vocation is to be made not so much in the self-expression of the individual personality as in his self-submission to the consecrated unity of the one worshipful life as that life is fulfilled in and through the many members. The life-vocation of each member is thus realized by his becoming an integral part of Christ's offering. For that which Jesus offers to the Father is the harmony of many responses in one, that one response which all offer in him. This is the underlying implication of all that is said in the argument of 1 Corinthians 12–14.[4] The sacrificial character of Christ's Body in all its aspects is so constantly emphasized by St Paul that the hymn in praise of love (Ch. 13) must be understood to have this implication. It carries the argument forward, linking together Chapters 12 and 14. For here we pass from the unity of a bodily organism to the problem of personal relationships. Unity at the human level involves 'mutual submission' as it is called in another epistle,[5] or again the mutual 'edification' which is specially emphasized in Chapter 14. Here the Corinthian Christians are invited to subordinate their natural desire for self-expression to the common life of the church.

[1] Prov. 8[22].

[2] cp. 1 Cor. 1[23]–2[16], 2 Cor. 5[14, 15], Eph. 2[13–22].

[3] Eph. 4[7].

[4] This becomes clear on a wider survey of the epistle as a whole, and especially of Chs. 8–11, culminating in the scandal of selfish disorder in the sacramental commemoration of Christ's sacrifice.

[5] Eph. 5[21].

vi

In 1 Cor. 14 'structure' imagery is supplemented by musical analogy with a scriptural background. In 14[7, 8] notes are distinct parts of an ordered whole. In Psalm 19[1-4] the 'parts' are speechless movements; in Wisdom 19[18] *ff* the ' parts' are elements remaining distinct, yet co-ordinated. In the church a babel of speech would contradict the witness of the *kosmos* to the Creator, by contrast with the new song of Zion (Isaiah 34, 35) which presupposes ordered 'understanding'. A modern parallel to this.

The emphasis on 'edification' in 1 Corinthians 14 is very marked, occurring as it does no less than seven times in verses 3–26. The Greek words employed, like their Latin and English equivalents, convey the double suggestion of a spiritual process manifested in the 'build up' of a structural form. The context might suggest that we have thus passed from the body image to that of a temple; and it is worthy of notice that in Ephesians 2 and 4 the two images have coalesced in such a way that there it is the body which is being built up.[1] This combination is probably implicit in the earlier epistle; but even so the reality with which the apostle is dealing transcends all such images of structure. Something else is required which will illustrate the problem of personal co-operation. So St Paul introduces a musical analogy from verse 7 onwards. As he proceeds it would appear that he has in mind, not simply a satisfying performance on a single instrument, but something having a more corporate character. The trumpet mentioned in verse 8 summons an army to battle; and this is only one of several sorts of summons mentioned in Numbers 10[1] *ff* to which the congregation of Israel are to make the appropriate response. One naturally thinks of an orchestra responding jointly to the baton of the conductor, who, in turn, interprets the mind of the composer. We must beware, however, of reading into the apostle's mind the technique of modern orchestral music. The language employed suggests strongly a scriptural background which points us away to the order of creation.

In 14[2-9] the unintelligible sounds of 'speaking with tongues' are compared to the indistinct or uncertain sound of a trumpet

---

[1] Eph. 2[14-22], 4[11-16].

which has its notes blurred, so that the signal made is unintelligible. By contrast the preceding verse states that if the air or tune played on a musical instrument is to be recognized the sound of each note must be distinguishable from those which precede and follow. The sequence becomes intelligible if the identity and contribution of each individual note is preserved; but not otherwise (14^7). Here we have a conception of an ordered whole in which the parts remain distinct while entering into combination. If this be compared with the opening verses of Psalm 19 a certain correspondence may be observed. In the Hebrew text 'the heavens' are likened to a choir singing the praises of the Creator. Yet 'there is neither speech nor language; their voice cannot be heard'.[1] The ordered combination of astronomical movements bears witness to divine power and wisdom. If St Paul had this psalm in mind, as seems possible,[2] it can be assumed that he found in it an analogue to the new creation, in which the parts combine to express the purpose of the whole, namely due acknowledgment of the Creator. There is, however, another possibility. In Wisdom $19^{18\,ff}$ the author uses a musical illustration to explain the plagues of Egypt, where the elements of nature co-operated with the Creator's redemptive purpose.

In verse 18 he remarks that 'as the notes of a psaltery vary the character of the rhythm, even so did the elements, changing their order one with another, continuing always the same, each in its several sound'. The main point of the analogy here is that individual units without change of their essential nature can, by combination with other units of like status, contribute to the production of a new 'order'. So in the Corinthian church distinct words combined in an orderly way could contribute to the edification of all present. The apostle's thought is further developed[3] through the medium of a quotation from Isaiah $28^{11,\,12}$. From this he concludes that a confused babel of glossolaly could be impressive only to those who have not yet come to believe in a Creator-God calling into existence the harmony of the *kosmos*.

[1] 19^3 (H 19^4). Briggs *ad loc.* in ICC suggests that this verse is a 'prosaic' gloss to explain the poetic paradox of the original, i.e. speechless praise rendered by movements which conform to the Creator's will.

[2] His language in $14^{7,\,10}$ may echo the LXX text (Ps. $18^{4,\,5}$) which by-passes the 'prosaic gloss'.

[3] I Cor. $14^{21\,ff}$.

We may compare the dolorous drone of the false prophets in 1 Kings 22⁶, the typically 'totalitarian' kakophony of a servile mob. The apostle, however, sees a worse possibility. If such kakophony occurs in the church an unbeliever, if present, would see in it a sign of madness, and rightly so. For such an assembly would represent nothing at all, neither the harmonies of heaven, nor the accepted blare of a barbaric paganism. It would be the discord of a perverted spirituality.

It is important to remember that the argument of 1 Corinthians 14 is not directed against 'speaking with tongues' as such, but against its anti-social use for unedifying self-display in the common life.[1] This has, in the apostle's mind, further implications to which we shall return presently. Meanwhile let us take note that in this phase of his discourse he has passed from the image of a single bodily organism to a more general principle of order, and that his musical illustration fits readily onto a scriptural background which finds the witness of creation to its Creator in its orderly multiform response to his will. The speechless voices of creation are not dumb. They make ineffable music to their Creator, as they answer his call. If we do not hear or heed their testimony that is, perhaps, because we ourselves are to some extent deafened by our own discordant cries. The difference between such a confusion of tongues in our modern Babel and the new song of the heavenly Zion[2] is foreshadowed in the prophetic contrasts of Isaiah 34 and 35. In the first of these two scenes pandemonium is let loose upon the ruins of an accursed city where 'the howling creatures' foregather and 'the satyr' cries to his fellow (34¹⁴). In the second scene the ears of the deaf are unstopped, as though to hear celestial harmonies when 'the tongue of the dumb shall sing'. The wild beasts have disappeared; and their harsh cries are replaced by the song of the redeemed, as Israel 'returns' to the Lord in Zion to make melody in his holy temple (35⁶⁻¹⁰).

If we set St Paul's argument on to a scriptural background as indicated above, we can see how significantly he has brought out the difference between the harmonies of the new creation and 'the music of the spheres'. The new song of Zion is not a 'natural' effect of creation like the song of the speechless choir in Psalm 19. It may be compared to the song which 'the morning

[1] See further my *Confirmation*, Ch. 3, § iv.   [2] Rev. 14¹⁻³, 15²⁻⁴.

stars sang together' when the foundations of the earth were laid
(Job 38[7]); for the parallel line in that verse identifies the stars
with 'the sons of God' who shouted for joy.[1] If, however, the
new song is to be heard in its full beauty, every human faculty
must be consecrated and so bend itself to the task. It is not sufficient for 'the spirit' to pray, if 'the understanding' remains 'un-
fruitful' (14[14 ff]). Thus the apostle insists that mutual edification involves mutual understanding. If we turn to a modern
version of the musical analogy, orchestral music illustrates the
point. Only a long educational discipline and unceasing prac-
tice will enable the performers under the leadership of a good
conductor to express worthily the mind of the composer. Moreover, besides and behind all this there lies also the specialized
training and tradition of those who make and produce musical
instruments as well as the planning and co-operation which win
the best results from their skilled labour. The 'things without
life' which men make for such a purpose are the product of
creative thought and subserve mutual understanding.[2] They
thus typify members of Christ's body who are instrumental to
the edification of the church, because all their powers of mind
and body serve the common life as that life is offered in Jesus to
the Father.

vii

The relation of 'understanding' (*nous*) to 'innocence' (1 Cor.
14[20]) and to 'simplicity' (2 Cor. 11[2, 3]) in the cosmic harmonies
of the new creation. *Nous*, the ruling faculty in man, loses control
of the 'members' through high-mindedness. So Romans 7 repeats
Genesis 3. Yet by 'the mind of Christ' (1 Cor. 2[16]) the lost dominion is restored in Jesus the Servant and in his members, with
transforming effects, Godward and manward, in the relationships
of redeemed humanity.

In our analysis of 1 Corinthians 14 nothing has as yet been
said concerning verse 20, which runs as follows: 'Brethren, be
not children in mind; but in malice be babes and in mind be per-

---

[1] The attribution of angelic personality to the stars is not apparently con-
fined to this text in scripture. See *Revelation*, p. 210, note 1, and p. 214.

[2] 1 Cor. 14[7, 9, 12-19].

fect.' The final word implies the mature judgement of full-grown men, and is contrasted with childishness as in $3^{1, 2}$ of this same epistle. But there is a notable difference of language between the two passages. There the immature Christians are called 'babes', whereas here they are exhorted to be 'babes' in the sense of childlike innocence with regard to all that is evil. 'Babes' in this good sense correspond to the 'little children' of our Lord's teaching, and again to that 'simplicity' which the apostle recommended in 2 Corinthians $11^{2, 3}$, and which we compared to the 'single eye' in our Lord's teaching.[1] This is the simplicity of the new Adam which he imparts to his bride, the new Eve, that she may continue to be truly 'joined' to her divine spouse. This word used by St Paul in the last-mentioned passage to express this ideal union corresponds (in its spelling) to our word 'harmonize', and may even have carried that meaning. The union of Christ and his bride is ideally one in which the 'adornment' of the bride corresponds to the cosmic harmonies of the new creation.[2] In 1 Corinthians 14^{20} the alternative biblical image for 'simplicity' is employed; and the innocence of babes here recalls an alternative picture of cosmic harmony in the song of the first creation (Psalm 8).[3]

In that psalm the cosmic choir is no longer speechless; for its praises are led by the 'babes and sucklings' who are Adam's children. These, in fact, combine innocence with the beginnings of 'understanding', and as such provide a type of what the apostle has in mind, when he recommends his readers to combine childlike innocence with maturity of judgement. Here there is no room for either sentimentalism or self-display. Harmonious co-operation in the structure of the new creation depends upon mutual 'understanding' through the consecration of all human faculties to the service of God in Christ. Now the word here rendered 'understanding' (*nous*) in verses 14–19 is used elsewhere by St Paul for the judgement by which we approve a right course of action, even though, through moral weakness, we are unable to follow it (Romans 7^{22-25}). That power of the mind, which might promote the edification of the Christian community by fostering mutual understanding, might

---

[1] See above, Ch. II, § v, pars. 4.*ff.*
[2] cp. above, § i, par. 2, and, for 'adornment', 1 Pet. $3^{3, 4}$.
[3] For which see *Dominion*, Ch. III, from p. 73 onwards.

also, under God, build up the moral integrity of the individual by regulating the complex forces of his nature. Such unification of man, however, is frustrated. The ruling faculty does not rule; and this paralysis of the higher self is due to a false independence which separates man from God.

Here we see in the individual the repetition of Adam's story. *Nous*, the ruling faculty in man, loses its rightful dominion over the other 'members'[1] of the individual *kosmos*, just as Adam lost his rightful dominion over the other creatures in the first creation. The parallel with Adam has already appeared in Romans 7^{11}, where sin plays the part of the serpent.[2] Man was made in God's image that he might partake of the divine wisdom, and so co-operate with the Creator's purpose. In fallen man this creative capacity of the mind remains; but now, through pride and self-will, it works destructively for its own ends. Instead of building up it pulls down.[3] In Christ, however, we have access once more to all the treasures of the divine wisdom.[4] For 'who knew the mind of the Lord that he should instruct him? But we have the mind of Christ'. Here, in 1 Corinthians 2^{16}, quoting Isaiah 40^{13} from the Septuagint, St Paul uses the word *nous* twice. As the beloved Son, Jesus is the *divine* counsellor of the Father. But as the second Adam he is also the *human* counsellor for deity, of whom no trace could be found in his day by the prophet whom St Paul is quoting.[5] But thirdly, since he is Wisdom incarnate, Jesus is the *divine-human* counsellor[6] who, sharing the creative thought of the Father, co-operates with him as Head of Adam's restored dominion.

Into this restored dominion Jesus has summoned us by his creative call, that we, through union with him, may partake of his thoughts and thus share his high-priestly functions on behalf of creation. To answer this call is to partake in 'the obedience of the Christ'; and this, in turn, involves a sharing of his conflict

---

[1] With μέλη twice in Rom. 7^{23} cp. its occurrence four times in Rom. 6^{12-19} and three times in Rom. $12^{4, 5}$. Cp. also 1 Cor. 12^{12-27}, and see below, pars. 4 fol.

[2] cp. Gen. 3^{13}, 2 Cor. 11^3. The parallel goes back to Rom. $5^{12\,ff}$.

[3] cp. 2 Cor. 10^8, and see below, § viii, par. 1.

[4] Col. 2^3.

[5] In Isa. 40^{13} the Hebrew phrase rendered 'counsellor' means literally 'man of his counsel'.

[6] cp. Prov. $8^{22\,ff}$, and above, § i, par. 2.

with evil. Baptism meant for us a change of allegiance. We passed from the service of Sin to the service of Righteousness. By the divine act of justification we were then clothed with the righteousness of Christ. We entered upon that way of obedience which Jesus fulfilled in his great act of redress to the Father. Thus we, 'the many', became members of the One righteous Man; and because we are *his* members we are to present *our* members in him to the Father, that they may become weapons in the divine hand, consecrated for use in the holy war against sin (Romans 5[18]–6[19]). In this argument it is presupposed that Jesus is the second Adam because he fulfils the Servant prophecy (4[25]–5[11]).[1] Moreover, in accordance with Isaiah 49[2], the Servant's members are included in the divine armoury. Thus, there is a double submission involved for us. As an athlete brings all the 'members' of his body under control, so a Christian must bring all the capacities of his nature into subordination to Christ's obedience. But this implies also mutual submission of all the members to one another in Christ, that there may be formed in them one mind and purpose to the greater glory of God.[2]

In all this we see the triadic character of the new creation made luminously clear. The sober estimate of ourselves recommended by St Paul in Romans 12 would enable us to play our parts humbly in Christ's body as 'members one of another', each making precisely that contribution which corresponds to the gift bestowed upon him. This sober estimate of ourselves, however, is the fruit of a transforming process in which the mind is renewed through entire self-oblation towards God (12[1, 2]).[3] By such a renewal of the ruling faculty (*nous*) a death-blow is struck at 'high-mindedness', which is here seen to be the chief obstacle to a clear apprehension *both* of the divine will *and* of our neighbour's need. In this picture the lowly obedience of Jesus[4] is reproduced in his members; and in Chapter 13 its fruits are manifested in the wider sphere of social order. For 'the obedience of the Christ' fulfils the whole law by including the second

---

[1] Just as 1 Cor. 15[1–4] is presupposed in the first appearance of the second Adam doctrine at 15[22].

[2] We can now see that this is the underlying theme of 1 Cor. 14[20–40]. Cp. especially vv. 31–33 and the conclusion of v. 25. For 'mutual submission' (Eph. 5[21]) see above, § v, concluding sentences.

[3] cp. above, Ch. I, § vii, par. 1.　　　　　　　[4] cp. Phil. 2[8].

'duty' in the first.[1] Just so far then as, by putting on 'the Lord Jesus Christ', we participate in his obedience, we fulfil in both spheres of duty the functions proper to our vocation; and this fulfilment is the 'reasonable worship' (12^1) which is acceptable to God. Thus we may summarize the teaching of Romans 12 and 13.

viii

A campaign for total surrender to Christ (2 Cor. 10^{3-6} in contrast to Rom.7). Lowly submission to him creates a new level of Christian fellowship and mutual understanding. Response to the creative call involves mutual submission in the temple of the body, with unchanging significance, however varied the conditions. Three gospel parables illustrate this fact. Divine and human standards concerning 'equalities' are incommensurate. Yet revolution in the human sphere is effected by the new order in Christ.

The harmony of Christ's body is endangered by high-mindedness, but built up by mutual submission. For the peace of God's city is grounded upon that great act of humiliation which is summed up in the apostolic phrase: 'the obedience of the Christ.' The phrase occurs in full in 2 Corinthians 10^5; and the context in which it occurs will throw further light upon its relation to Pauline thought as a whole. As in Romans, so here, the ideas belonging to this theme are expressed in terms of military metaphor.[2] When fallen man gives his allegiance to Christ, he yields up his sovereign rights. Yet there may remain in his nature tracts of unsubdued territory which have not yet surrendered. These are like fortresses isolated by the advance of a victorious army. They may represent a relatively small portion of the conquered territory. But for all that they impair the completeness of the surrender; and their reduction is indispensable. Such rebellious strongholds must be demolished. Yet the defence is stubborn; for the defenders construct and throw up a variety of defence-mechanisms with skill born of long experience.

A parallel may here be drawn with the picture in Romans

---

[1] Mark 12^{28-33}.
[2] cp. 2 Cor. 10^{3-6} with Rom. 6^{12-19} and 7^{23}.

7^{15-25}.[1] There the ruling faculty in the apostle's nature was taken captive and enslaved to sin. This happened through the rebellious conduct of his 'members',[2] that is his subordinate faculties. Their leader[3] was thus made an unwilling, but helpless, prisoner, who accordingly welcomed with gratitude the deliverance effected by Christ when sin was finally dethroned. In 2 Corinthians 10^{1-6} the situation is different. St Paul is here a captain in Christ's army conducting a difficult campaign for the reduction of enemy strongholds in the church of Corinth In this scene, therefore, the powers of the human mind are by no means unwilling captives; for they are actively engaged in opposition to the gospel. Nevertheless these powers are God-given and must not be destroyed. Though they have gone over to the enemy they must be rescued from their false allegiance. Every mental project emanating from such a source must be captured and brought back into that sphere, here designated 'the obedience of the Christ', to which man's true and total allegiance properly belongs. For the sphere of Christian allegiance is precisely that obedience which 'the One Man Jesus Christ' offered on behalf of 'the many'. He did so in order that the many, as his members, might offer the same obedience in him.[4] Our obedience, therefore, is a participation in his,—in that which he renders to the Father; and this participation is shared equally by all the members of Christ's body. Thus our obedience is to be fulfilled, not *in vacuo*, but by each through all his brethren; and this involves mutual submission.

The rule that we are to submit ourselves to one another 'in the fear of Christ'[5] gives to all social relationships a religious significance. One of its implications stands out in Romans 14^4 which reminds us that every Christian is the Lord's servant,

---

[1] See above, § vii, pars. 2*ff*; and cp. the verbal similarity of Rom. 7^{23} (νοῦς) and 2 Cor. 10^5 (νόημα), with the same verb for 'taking captive' representing, however, an opposite situation.

[2] Note the Hebrew idiom. A bodily term stands for a psychological factor cp. Matt. $6^{22, 23}$.

[3] The true self is identified with νοῦς, which, even as sin's captive, does not cease to be God's servant (7^{25}).

[4] Rom. $5^{18, 19}$, 2 Cor. $5^{14, 15}$. Cp. again the similarities between 2 Cor. $10^{5, 6}$ and Rom. 5^{19}. 2 Cor. 10^3 differentiates Gal. 2^{20} from Rom. 8^4 (use of σάρξ); and 2 Cor. 10^{3-6} anticipates, at least verbally, some of the main themes of Rom. $5^{15}-8^{13}$.

[5] Eph. 5^{21}.

answerable, therefore, to the Lord, and not primarily to the *individual* judgement of his fellow-Christians.[1] In our common submission to the Lord Christ we stand together beneath him, and all on the same lowly level. Thus the New Jerusalem fulfils the prophecy which proclaims the exaltation of Mount Zion, as the *locus* of the divine presence, 'at the top of the mountains' and 'above the hills'. We belong to that new day of the Lord which, once for all, levelled all 'the high places' of the idols, the day which brought low the lofty and exalted the humble.[2] For it is 'he that humbleth himself' who 'shall be exalted'.[3] The humiliation of Jesus deflated all human claims to superiority; and his exaltation created a new equality of all men in him. The new level upon which we all stand might be described as the exalted level of Christ's lowliness. So, too, the medium through which we are to approach our fellow men is 'the meekness and consideration of the Christ'.[4] The meekness in which we here participate effects in us such a submission of our cause to God as to remove all grounds for resentment towards our fellows. This, in turn, enables us to consider their claims, their convictions, their points of view with that fairness which is demanded by their relation to Christ. Mutual submission, so understood, is a work of mutual understanding in which the removal of high-mindedness opens up continually new vistas of insight into the divine likeness in our fellow-men.

Equal honour is accorded to all members of Christ's body, since all fulfil functions which are equally necessary to the whole. Moreover, for their diverse functions in the body the members are equipped with corresponding gifts which are divinely bestowed.[5] In the various statements of the 'body' doctrine, indeed, nothing is said concerning the relation between gifts of the Spirit (*charismata*) and natural endowments. Two things, however, are clear: first, that we have nothing which we have not received from God;[6] and secondly, that by the creative call of God we were summoned into the path of Christ's obedience. Response to the call, therefore, involves our placing all the

---

[1] cp. Rom. 14[10-12]. The corporate judgement of the church is, of course, on an altogether different footing.

[2] Isa. 2[2, 10-18]; cp. 40[4].   [3] Luke 14[11], Matt. 23[12].

[4] 2 Cor. 10[1] (M).

[5] 1 Cor. 12[4-11], Rom. 12[6]; Eph. 4[7], 1 Pet. 4[10].   [6] 1 Cor. 4[7].

resources of our being at the disposal of him who created them, in order that they may be moulded to the form of the Servant. The process of mutual submission is fundamental to this response. For we are built into the temple of the body as 'living stones' which, by submission to the builder's blows are so shaped as to fit into one another in that living whole wherein sanctuary and sacrifice are one (Ephesians 4$^{15, 16}$, 1 Peter 2$^{4-10}$). In both of these passages the sacrificial note is struck. We become a 'holy priesthood' by coming to the rejected stone; and this we can do only 'in love'.

From this analysis it appears that vocation in Christ and man's response thereto always have the same fundamental significance, no matter how diverse and unequal are the conditions under which these take place. This conclusion also corresponds broadly to the teaching given by our Lord in his parables of service and reward. If, for example, comparisons are made between three such parables the variations are sufficiently striking: (1) In Luke 19$^{12-27}$ ('the pounds') the servants are entrusted with identically the same tasks, achieve unequal results, and receive correspondingly unequal rewards. (2) In Matthew 25$^{14-30}$ ('the talents') the servants are set unequal tasks, but according to their individual ability. Likewise they attain unequal results, but in proportion to the tasks assigned to them. Finally, their reward is one in essence (the joy of their Lord), but turns out to be different in detail (verse 28). These two parables are also identical in their conclusion. The unused money is handed over to the man who attained the maximum results. (3) In Matthew 20$^{1-16}$ ('the vineyard') the story of the pounds is reversed. For here the labourers are called to unequal tasks, and necessarily achieve unequal results; yet all receive the same reward. To these details two comments may be added. Whatever be the actual history of (1) and (2), they now embody quite different ideas, notwithstanding the identity of the concluding utterance in them both. On the other hand, the more complex scheme of (2) mediates between (1) and (3), as the diagram opposite shows.

Yet in each of these stories, despite all differences of detail, an unexpected ending fixes the attention upon a contrast between divine and human judgements concerning equality and inequality, between the divine order of vocation and response, on

	pounds Lk. 19[12-27]	talents Mt. 25[14-30]	vineyard Mt. 20[1-16]
tasks	the same	unequal (according to ability)	unequal
results	unequal	unequal (but in pro- portion)	unequal
rewards	unequal (but in pro- portion) yet	the same (in essence) but unequal in detail	the same
To everyone that hath shall be given, and from him that hath not . . .	proportional inequality is over- thrown by a law of increasing and decreasing returns		Cp. Rom. 6[23] Mt. 25[29] = Lk. 19[26]

the one hand, and human standards of justice on the other. The two spheres are strictly incommensurate. Considerations which are all-important in the one are simply irrelevant in the other. But further, it is to be noticed that in the New Testament human inequalities, as such, are never the direct object of interest. Examples could be multiplied. Our Lord refused to adjudicate in a matter of human justice, but made the incident an occasion for a homily on covetousness.[1] The Epistle to Philemon is concerned, not with slavery as such, but with brotherly love. St Paul regards differences of social status as matters of indifference by comparison with the new status in Christ.[2] He does not directly envisage a change in current conventions on such matters as the social relationships between members of the same family or household.[3] Nevertheless, in spite of this pre-occupation with the new order in Christ and this detachment from purely human interests as such, a profound revolution is already taking place in the human sphere.

[1] Luke 12[13-21].
[2] 1 Cor. 7[17-24]; cp. Gal. 3[28].
[3] Col. 3[18]-4[1] illustrates this sentence; and its context (e.g. 3[5-17]) illustrates what here follows.

Of this a single instance will suffice. St Paul assumes without question the headship of man over woman. But his treatment of this subject brings it into relation with mysteries which will inevitably transform it.[1] For 'if one member is honoured, all the members rejoice with it',[2] and that *because* they are members of one body in Christ. Once more the threefold relationship takes effect in the submission of all to Christ in his body and members. The inequalities which outrage a Christian sense of justice are, in their present form, a consequence of man's fallen condition. They represent, in fact, a perversion and distortion of differences in human nature which are, in themselves, good. For these differences underlie, and make possible, all those diversities of function which enrich society. The healing of such perversion, however, cannot lie in human justice; for that justice is itself corrupted at its source by original sin. The healing power can come only from the righteousness of God, embodied, manifested, operative, and therefore also vindicated in the new order of Christ. Of all this the visible church in her low estate can be no more than the effectual sign, pointing always towards the true form of society as an end attainable only in a worshipping and worshipful community such as the church herself is. For worship is the response which Christ offers to the Father, and which all men may offer in him. We are created for this response; and only therein can our nature find the significant and satisfying fulfilment alike of its diversities and of its unities.

[1] 1 Cor. 11$^{3-12}$. Such development is already evident in Eph. 5$^{21-33}$, where the subject is vitally connected with mutual submission.
[2] 1 Cor. 12^{26}.

CHAPTER IV

CREATION AND WORSHIP

i

Function of the visible church as 'sign' of salvation and judgement through union with Christ, the all-sufficient 'sign of Jonah'. He is the 'sign spoken against', whose lot is shared alike by mother and bride in fulfilment of Israel's destiny as co-partner in the plan of redemption. So in NT the part of 'New Eve' belongs to the church and to the Mother of Jesus, and to both in the Apocalypse. 'The seed of the woman' and Emmanuel in Revelation 12.

In the preceding volume of this series our starting point was the apostolic conviction that Christ is the sphere in which the secrets of creation become manifest.[1] From this we have proceeded eventually to what may be regarded as a corresponding truth, namely, that the church visible here on earth is the 'effectual sign' of our Lord's present glory and of man's true home and destiny. On the other hand, it has also become clear that the 'sign' so given has two contrasted aspects. The glory of the Lamb is inseparable from his obedience. The scars in the flesh of Jesus mark the sphere of our present conflict. Accordingly, to enter the heavenly city is to share the descent of the city, by the lowly track of Christ's obedience, into the place of that conflict. Thus the 'sign' is 'effectual' because it makes accessible to us, and in us, that which it signifies or reveals. It is two-sided because, as the vehicle of God's gracious call, it summons men to a difficult response. It is at once the place of salvation and also the place of trial and judgement. The visible church, in and through which the city of God descends to earth, is a sign which has this double character. But it has such significance solely as the bearer of the Lamb. For Christ alone is God's completely effectual sign in which all others are comprehended, or to which at least their significance must be referred.

[1] *Dominion*, Ch. I, § i.

So when the Jews demanded from Jesus 'a sign from heaven'
he refused to give it (Mark 8¹¹⁻¹³). Instead he offered them 'the
sign of Jonah' as fulfilled in himself. For he not only called men
to repentance, as Jonah did (Luke 11²⁹⁻³²). He also embodied
the divine message to man, sealing it and fulfilling it in his death
and resurrection, as (in a figure) Jonah had done (Matthew
12³⁸⁻⁴¹). Now the church is one with Jesus in that fulfilment.
Consequently she also shares the dread agony prophetically
assigned by Simeon to the Mother of Jesus when he held her
child in his arms:

> Behold this child is set for the falling and rising up of many in
>   Israel,
> and for a sign which is spoken against;
> Yea, and a sword shall pierce through thine own soul,
> that thoughts out of many hearts may be revealed (Luke 2³⁴, ³⁵).

These words were addressed to the mother of the Messiah, that
is to say, to the human agent who, on behalf of mankind,
accepted God's gift of his only Son (Luke 1³⁸). As such, Mary
fulfilled the destiny of old Israel; and in so doing she also provided the indispensable link with the corresponding destiny of
the new Israel. In her freely willed acceptance of the Incarnation she fulfilled Israel's vocation to co-operate with the Creator.
Moreover, that co-operation was indispensable, since man is
God's viceroy over creation. The part thus assigned to the
human race is integral to the divine plan of creation, and therefore also, and equally, to the divine plan of redemption.

The mother, therefore, was the necessary counterpart of her
child; and in that respect she foreshadowed the destiny of the
church as the bride of Christ. The blessed Virgin was the indispensable partner of the Creator in his inauguration of the new
creation, as the new Israel is the equally indispensable partner
of the Messiah in its consummation. This double truth links
together the mother of Jesus and his bride in one common
vocation. It also explains the fact that, whereas from the first the
apostolic interpretation found in the church a new Eve corresponding to the new Adam, there are also distinct indications
that, from another point of view, a counter-part of Eve was discerned in the Virgin-mother of the Christ. The former interpretation is explicit in 2 Corinthians 11², ³, where characteristi-

cally the local church represents the church universal.[1] The
more elaborate treatment of this theme in Ephesians 5$^{22-33}$
exhibits a typically biblical kind of symbolism which may serve
to prepare the mind for the alternative interpretation in its
characteristically Johannine forms.[2] Moreover, a further connecting link is provided by the fact that in the Revelation of St
John both interpretations appear.

To one of these our own second chapter was largely devoted.
In Chapters 19–22 the church as bride is the partner of Christ's
rule and the sphere of its exercise.[3] The image of the descending
city, however, makes its first appearance as early as Revelation
3^{12}. It is, therefore, already in the author's mind before he
reaches the alternative image in Chapter 12, where he describes
his vision of the 'woman clothed with the sun' who is the mother
of the Messiah. In the record of this vision and in its sequel we
see the fulfilment of two classic utterances from the Old Testament. The first of these is the promise contained in the words
addressed to the serpent after the Fall:

I will put enmity between thee and the woman, and between thy
seed and her seed: it shall bruise thy head, and thou shalt bruise his
heel (Genesis 3^{15}).[4]

Jesus is the promised seed of the woman; and the child-bearing
of Mary inaugurates the final stages of that conflict which began
so disastrously in Eden. To the scenes in this section of the
Apocalypse many Old Testament foreshadowings contribute.
But the basis of the seer's vision lies in a fusion of the promise
just cited from Genesis with a corresponding promise given by
the prophet Isaiah on the occasion of his meeting with King Ahaz.

In the form in which it is quoted in St Matthew's Gospel this
promise reads as follows:

Behold the virgin shall be with child and shall bear a son, and they
shall call his name Emmanuel (Matthew 1^{23}).

[1] On 1 Cor. 11$^{3\,ff}$ see above, Ch. I, § iii.

[2] For John 19$^{25-30}$ see above, Ch. I, § v, par. 5; and cp. *The Fourth Gospel*,
by Sir E. C. Hoskyns, Vol. II, pp. 631–634.

[3] cp. above, Ch. III, § i, par. 1, final note; and for a Jewish parallel see
2 (4) Esdras, 10$^{27,\,44}$.

[4] The narrative of Rev. 12$^{1-5}$, however, appears to correspond more
closely to the LXX version of Gen. 3^{15}, as I have indicated in *Dominion*,
p. 121 *f*. See also, *ib.* pp. 154.*ff*, and also my contribution to *The Mother of
God* (Dacre Press), pp. 19.*ff*.

We are here taken back to a distant episode in Israel's history.[1] The kingdom of Judah is threatened by enemies; but Isaiah assures the king that the threat will come to nothing. In proof of this he offers the king a 'sign' of his own choosing, saying: 'Make it deep unto Sheol or make it high upwards.' This might be paraphrased: 'Ask for anything in heaven or hell; for there is no limit to God's power.' Ahaz, however, refused the offer; for his mind was set upon worldly policies, whereas he should have remembered the 'signs and wonders' of the Exodus. Isaiah then substituted for his original offer the Emmanuel promise which has for us such strong associations with the Christmas story. Moreover, he introduced that promise with these words: 'The Lord himself shall give you a sign' (Isaiah 7[3-14]). We now have to see in what way these two basic promises of the old covenant find joint fulfilment in the vision of Revelation 12, and further what conclusions follow therefrom.

ii

Signs 'in heaven' blending Gen. 3[15] with Isa. 7[11, 14] correspond to the biblical fusion of messianic prophecy with 'new creation' themes. The 'great sign' set within the lights of the first creation is the New Eve-Israel divinely indwelt. Rev. 12[1-5] shows the two creations united in the New Adam who is Christ the Redeemer. The first creation foreshadows the second; but the new order is fulfilled only within the old. The new luminary is Eve-Israel-Mary creatively 'called out' to bring forth Messiah.

In Revelation 12 the vision of the woman with child opens with these words: 'And there appeared a great sign in heaven.' The phraseology certainly appears to reflect Isaiah 7[14]; for that is the only biblical passage where such a sign is promised.[2] This,

[1] For full details of criticism and interpretation see Gray on Isaiah Chs. i–xxvii in ICC *ad loc.*, and *The Sign of Immanuel* by Prof. S. H. Hooke in *Sobornost*, The Journal of the Fellowship of S. Alban and S. Sergius, Series 3: No. 16.

[2] The word for 'sign' in Rev. 12[1, 3] is the word usually employed in LXX for signs sent by God. It is so used in the story of the Exodus, where Moses and Aaron perform signs which are at first imitated by the magicians. In Rev. 15[1] the sign 'great and marvellous' of angels bearing the seven last plagues corresponds to the plagues of Egypt (cp. v. 3). Moreover, here too a false prophet, as in Egypt, performs signs before the Beast (13[13, 14], 19[20]).

however, is not 'a sign *from* heaven' (such as the Jews demanded
from Jesus) to compel belief. Rather is it, like the vision of the
New Jerusalem, a mystery of faith unveiled to the eye of the
believing Christian seer. It is 'a sign *in* heaven'; and it is followed immediately by 'another sign in heaven', namely, the
great dragon who stood before the woman, that when her child
was born he might devour it (verses 3, 4). It also appears that in
these four verses (1–4) we have a double conjunction of biblical
images. For, in the first place, the sign of the woman with child
and a corresponding sign of the dragon are brought together
into one picture in accordance with the promise that the seed of
the woman would bruise the serpent's head. But, secondly, these
two contrasted signs are both set 'in the heaven'; and this
reminds us of the challenge to King Ahaz: 'Make it deep . . . or
make it high.' Thus, in the conjunction of the two promises
from Genesis and Isaiah the prophet's two distinct offers to
Ahaz are also merged together. Both the signs are 'made high',
that is, set 'in the heaven'. But the second sign comes from the
'deep' of hell, whereas the first, the 'great sign', might be said
to come from 'on high'.

This fusion of the two prophetic backgrounds in Genesis and
Isaiah recalls the corresponding biblical fusion of messianic prophecy with 'new creation' themes, especially in this very book
of Isaiah.[1] Consequently it is natural to connect the great sign
of Revelation 12[1] with the creation of the sun, the moon and the
stars to be for 'signs' 'in the firmament of the heaven' (Genesis
1[14–18]). In the first creation the heavenly bodies were ordained
as 'signs' to give light. But there are numerous biblical passages
which predict the transformation of these signs in the last times.[2]
Moreover, in Luke 21[25] these transformations are described as
'signs *in* sun, moon and stars'. This gospel phrase corresponds
precisely to the spectacle which we are considering, where, however, the foreshadowings are surpassed in the fulfilment. For
here there are not many signs but one, the great sign to which
all others refer. This sign is '*in* sun and moon and stars', since
the woman with child is clothed with the sun, and has the moon

---

[1] The language of Rev. 12[5a] is taken from Isa. 66[7] and Ps. 2[9] (LXX). But
it also fits Isa. 11[4], which is followed by new creation details and cannot be
sharply separated from Isa. 7[14] in a NT context.

[2] cp. RV reff. under Luke 21[25].

under her feet; moreover, about her head is a crown of twelve stars. These represent the twelve tribes in accordance with Joseph's dream (Genesis 37⁹); for the woman is Israel as well as the New Eve. But that is only one aspect. God covers himself 'with light as with a garment' (Psalm 104²); and so it is here. The woman clothed in light is in travail with the divine child, Emmanuel. In her body God our Saviour becomes present with us.[1]

In the last chapter (§ iii) we found that God's 'covenant of the day . . . and of the night', maintained through the ordered movements of the heavenly bodies, both supports and also illuminates his later covenants in Israel and the new creation. The two orders mutually reinforce one another because both point to the same God.[2] So it was appropriate that the 'great sign' of the new creation, marking the rise of him who is both sun of righteousness and morning star,[3] should appear 'in the heaven' where the signs of the first creation are seen. The greatness of this sign, however, consists—in part, at least—in the fact that therein the two creations are united, since here the mother of Emmanuel is enshrined within those other signs of the first creation. The fulfilment of the messianic hope is set in a cosmic frame; and this aptly symbolizes the truth that the plan of the Creator is one, and that it is wholly Christological. But secondly, this sign indicates the fulfilment of the old order in the new. By virtue of the dominion granted to him Adam was, so to speak, the hub of creation. The representation, therefore, of the New Eve in childbirth as *the* sign in sun, moon and stars, sets the promised seed of the woman in the position from which Adam fell. In Psalm 8 a 'son of Adam' has 'the moon and the stars' as the background of his glory and of his dominion over the beasts; and this picture (as well as that in Daniel 7) is fulfilled in Revelation Chs. 12–20.

In the third place the seed of the woman, that is the Christ, is thus set in Adam's place at the centre of creation by virtue of his predestined rôle as the redeemer who bruises the serpent's head.

[1] As in 21² (of the bride), so here, the author may have read the vision concerning the mother set in 'a world-order' in the light of Isa. 61¹⁰ LXX, where the bridal adornment of Israel is a *kosmos*.

[2] cp. the twofold witness of the sabbath, as stated in Exodus 31¹²⁻¹⁸, on which see *Dominion*, pp. 65 *ff*.

[3] Mal. 4², Rev. 22¹⁶.

This is pre-eminently the sign of redemption. In this sign, however, all other signs meet. When lights were ordained as signs of
the first creation:

> God set them in the firmament of the heaven to give light upon the
> earth, and to rule over the day and over the night, and to divide the
> light from the darkness (Genesis 1[17, 18]).

In fulfilling these functions the 'great lights' prefigured the truth
of which Zacharias sang:

> The dayspring from on high shall visit us,
> To shine upon them that sit in darkness
>   and in the shadow of death,
> To guide our feet into the way of peace
>   (Luke 1[78, 79]).

But the truth so foreshadowed could come to realization only
within that order of creation in which it was foreshadowed. For
*it is only within the functions of the first creation that the mission of the
redeemer and his new order can come to fruition.* Thus in the heaven
of the Apocalypse the great sign of the uncreated light confronts
the sign of hell's darkness within that same order of created light
into which the darkness has brought confusion.[1]

The last paragraph has brought us to yet another facet of this
many-sided mystery. The New Eve is here represented as a
'great light' in heaven *before the birth of her child.* The new
luminary is, from one point of view, Israel in travail with the
Messiah. For the new creation must be formed within the womb
of the first creation if it is to be brought to fruition. From
another point of view, however, the new luminary is the Mother
of Jesus. For the forming of the new within the old was effected
by the event of the Incarnation 'when the fulness of the time
was come'. Now as Mary and Israel are here identified in the
figure of the New Eve, so the birth of Jesus is here set within the
frame of Israel's whole story on the background of the first
creation. Accordingly, as God summoned into existence signs in
heaven 'to divide the light from the darkness', so also, at the

---

[1] While waiting for Messiah's birth, the dragon disarranges the order of
the stars. 'He cast them to the earth' (12[4]). Now the stars may be angels (see
above, Ch. III, § vi, last par. with note); and in view of the supra-historical
character of the symbolism (see next par. in text) the seer may have had in
mind the fall of angels in Gen. 6[1–5] as a distant prelude to the imminent war
in heaven (12[7–12]).

next stage, he summoned Israel into existence to be a luminary which could serve as a light-bearing sign, a focus of the uncreated light. This creative summons is intimately associated in scripture with the calling of Israel out of Egypt, when by sovereign acts of power God divided the sons of light from the sons of darkness.[1]

iii

The Exodus, as treated in scripture, illustrates the unity of creation and redemption. So also the new Exodus in Rev. 12. The creatures co-operate with the Creator in his plan of redemption (Wisdom 16–19). Redemptive signs point forward to the Christ; and analogy is transcended in a functional unity which is consummated in worship, witness the Psalter, the Song of the Three and Revelation 4, 5.

The analogy between the deliverance from Egypt and our redemption in Christ provides one of the main threads of continuity in the bible. Moreover the imagery of the Exodus story is often connected in scripture with that of the creation theme in ways which have the effect of integrating the story of redemption with the wider plan of the Creator.[2] In this respect Revelation 12 is thoroughly typical. The escape of the Holy Child, and afterwards of his mother (verses 4–6 and 13 ff), corresponds to the preservations of Moses from child-massacre and a tyrant's wrath (Exodus 1^{16}–2^{15}), and of Israel at the Red Sea.[3] Moreover, in the last-mentioned parallel we come upon another feature of the 'Exodus' theme which bears striking testimony to the unity of the two creations in what I have called 'the wider plan of the Creator'. In Revelation $12^{15, 16}$ the dragon, pursuing 'the woman who bore the man-child', cast out of his mouth water to overwhelm her in a flood. But 'the earth helped the woman' by opening 'her mouth' to receive the water, so that the dragon's attempt was defeated. The form of this statement seems to be taken from the story of rebels in the wilderness who

[1] Exod. 10^{21-23}, Wisd. 17^2–18^4.

[2] e.g. Ps. 74^{12-14} on which see *Dominion*, pp. 48, 158. This passage goes much further than a conjunction of parallel themes such as we find, e.g. in Ps. 136.

[3] The 'eagle's wings' in Rev. 12^{14} contain an echo of Exod. 19^4.

were swallowed up by the earth (Numbers 16$^{23-33}$); but the analogy is clearly that of the Red Sea crossing. The Israel of God, under both covenants, escapes the pursuing enemy through the co-operation of the earth with the Creator. The elements of nature support the divine plan of redemptive history.

In the Song of Deborah we read that 'the stars in their courses fought against Sisera'.[1] The stars were enlisted by their Creator to serve on the side of Israel against their enemies. Here too it was believed that the elements co-operated with the divine actions in history. The classic instances of such co-operation, however, are the marvellous works which accompanied the Exodus from Egypt and the entry of Israel into the promised land. The ten plagues, the Red Sea passage, the provision of manna and water in the wilderness, the 'signs and wonders' associated with the conquest of Canaan,—in all of these events, at the bidding of their Creator, the creatures played their several parts in the restoration of the divine order and in fulfilment of the divine plan. This interpretation is implicit in the Old Testament, and is clearly presupposed in some of the great prophecies which herald the new creation. In the Book of the Wisdom of Solomon its implications are clearly stated in a lively commentary upon the 'signs and wonders' of the Exodus and the wilderness wanderings. Thus in Chapter 16, verse 24, we read:

The creation, ministering to thee its maker, straineth its force against the unrighteous for punishment, and slackeneth it in behalf of them that trust in thee, for beneficence.

Further, it belongs to this author's thesis that the 'signs and wonders' through which Israel's redemption was accomplished involved a refashioning of 'the whole creation', so that each of the elements might fulfil the divine commandments (19^6). Moreover, as we have seen in another connexion,[2] the transformations thus effected are likened by the author to the changes which occur in the rendering of a musical composition, where the notes 'vary the character of the rhythm' although the individual identity of the notes remains unchanged. So, too, without change in the individual character of the elements, the order of their mutual relations underwent variation, that they might

[1] Judges 5^{20}; cp. also Joshua 10$^{11-14}$.
[2] Ch. III, § vi, pars. 2, 3.

the better subserve the divine purpose (19^{18}; cp. 16^{17-27}). This interpretation of the sacred history, again, lies behind the record of redemptive signs which confronts us in the New Testament. The signs of the new covenant fall mainly into two classes, namely the miraculous events of the gospel history and the sacramental events which characterize the common life of the new Israel. Before we consider these, however, attention may be drawn to three implications of the biblical doctrine of signs, as thus far developed.

(i) The 'signs and wonders' which accompanied the foundation epoch of Israel's history were events in creation signifying the redemptive purpose of the Creator, and effecting that purpose. God's gracious care for his people was both manifested and embodied in these signs, because in them the order of creation became instrumental to the order of redemption. In them the Creator was revealed as Redeemer. In this respect, therefore, these signs pointed forward to the Christ who became God's completely effectual sign. (ii) In these signs elements of nature and representatives of the animal creation submitted themselves obediently to the divine word and commandments. They became instrumental to the order of redemption by obeying the call of their Creator and by conforming themselves to the new rhythm which he ordained for them. The use of this musical analogy in the Book of Wisdom recalls what was said in the last chapter about its use by St Paul in 1 Corinthians 14. There it referred to the redeemed community and illustrated the analogy between the two creations in respect of their several responses to the divine call. We can now see, however, that the correspondence between the two creations in this respect goes beyond analogy. For, on the one hand, the response of the redeemed order can take place only within the response of the original creation; and, on the other hand, the response of this creation to its Creator is evoked within the plan of redemption. (iii) In the redemptive signs, therefore, the destinies of the two creations are fused together into one. The signs, in fact, signify the fundamental unity of creation and redemption. For they show the community of the redeemed moving forward to its destiny within that functional response of creation as a whole without which the redeemed order cannot come to fruition.[1]

---

[1] cp. above, § ii, last two pars.

The signs, however, point, not simply to the unity of the two orders, but also to the fact that this unity attains its consummation in worship. This is well brought out in the psalms of praise with which the Psalter concludes. The two orders are here seen as two choirs united in their rendering of obedience to the divine conductor, united, therefore, in one offering of praise to their Creator whose sovereignty they together acclaim. This is precisely what the redemptive signs imply. Moreover, the sequence of worship in these psalms foreshadows the majestic scenes of Revelation 4 and 5, where, it will be remembered, the unity of the two creations is consummated in the adoration offered 'unto him that sitteth on the throne and unto the Lamb'.[1] So the church was wisely guided to include the psalter in her worship together with the Song of the Three Holy Children which exhibits a similar structure.

iv

The 'signs and wonders' of the Exodus story have their counterparts in the new Exodus. But NT shows also contrast in Christ, the one wholly effectual sign. With the Pauline analogy between 'Exodus signs' and Christian sacraments (1 Cor. 10) gospel miracles and sacraments are set together on the same background; and in this conjunction fulfilment is both cosmic and Christological. In the new order the healing miracles show a sacramental quality (detailed indications in Mark 6^{30}–9^{32}), while sacraments signify and mediate the worshipful response of restored creation.

In the Old Testament the expression 'signs and wonders' refers predominantly to the miracles connected with the Exodus of Israel from Egypt, although sometimes, by implication, it seems to cover also such incidents as the provision of manna and water in the subsequent journey through the wilderness. Such an extended meaning of the expression, for example, seems to be implied in the resumé of Israel's early history given in Nehemiah 9 (verses 9–15). In the New Testament a corresponding reference to the Exodus and its wilderness sequel appears explicitly in St Stephen's speech in connexion with his use of the phrase

---

[1] For which see *Dominion*, pp. 195.*ff*.

'wonders and signs' (Acts 7³⁶). Moreover, the sentence immediately following implies that Jesus is the prophet foreshadowed by Moses in Deuteronomy 18¹⁵ ('like unto me'); and this again would suggest that the new Moses has also shewn signs and wonders as of old. Elsewhere in the Acts (with some slight variations of phraseology) it is expressly declared that signs and wonders were wrought, first by Jesus, and then by his apostles.[1] This favourite Lucan thesis that the Gospel story repeats itself in the church underlines the truth that in the Exodus of the new Israel Jesus and his people are one.[2]

Thus far we see analogy and continuity between old and new Israel. Yet there is another side to the picture which must also be considered. In the last four chapters of the Wisdom of Solomon a commentary upon the Exodus story is unfolded which makes an emphatic contrast between the divine judgements upon Egypt and the providential treatment of Israel. So also in Revelation 15 the seven last plagues of the new Exodus provide a grim background to the joy of the redeemed who 'sing the song of Moses the servant of God and the song of the Lamb'.[3] In the New Testament as a whole, however, there is contrast as well as continuity between the old and the new. In more ways than one the traditional theme of 'signs and wonders' has been transcended by the advent of the one completely effectual sign in the person of Christ. Thus, in the gospels the healing miracles of Jesus are not primarily 'signs' to induce belief, but saving acts of 'power' wherein God's mercy is shewn to sinful humanity. Moreover, even in the fourth gospel where 'signs' are given a new meaning the use of signs and wonders to induce belief is expressly repudiated by Jesus.[4]

Next let us notice that in 1 Corinthians 10 St Paul develops a new form of the analogy between 'Exodus signs' and their counterparts in the new Israel. Referring to Israel's passage through the Red Sea (Exodus 14) he says that 'they were all baptized unto Moses in the cloud and in the sea'. Moreover they all partook of 'the same spiritual meat' and 'the same spiritual drink', that is to say the manna and the water from the

---

[1] By Jesus, Acts 2²²; by apostles, 2⁴³, 5¹² in answer to 4³⁰, 14³, 15¹²; cp. 4¹⁶, ²² and Rom. 15¹⁹, 2 Cor. 12¹²; by Stephen, Acts 6⁸.

[2] *Dominion*, p. 24 and note.

[3] Rev. 15¹⁻⁶.   [4] John 4⁴⁸.

rock; and 'the rock was the Christ'. The context shews that the apostle is here making a parallel with the Christian sacraments of baptism and the eucharist; and the immediate object of the parallel drawn is to convey a warning against the unworthy use of such privileges. The Christian comment on the wilderness story has shifted the balance. Judgement may fall, not only upon those who oppose God's people, but also upon those who are within the covenant; and this, of course, corresponds to the persistent teaching of the prophets that salvation and judgement are alternative effects of God's saving acts of power. Finally the analogy thus drawn with the marvellous works of God in the Exodus story places the Christian sacraments on the same background as that to which in Acts St Luke refers the healing miracles of Jesus and his apostles.[1]

This drawing together of miracles and sacraments in the new covenant on to a single background of signs and wonders in Israel's story is a matter to which more detailed attention must now be given. For there are manifold indications in the gospels themselves pointing in the same direction. If, however, this line of thought is to be profitably pursued we must at this point recall certain conclusions already reached. First, then, the events of the Exodus are connected in scripture, not only with creation, but also with the hope of a new creation.[2] Redemption has thus a cosmic significance; and further, the fulfilment of messianic prophecy includes the restoration of Adam's dominion.[3] Lastly, the various signs of the new order, whatever be the precise mode of their signification, are all integrally related to God's one completely effectual sign which is the Christ.[4] The whole of this complex of ideas is present in the New Testament and carries with it two further factors: (1) The healing miracles which signify the integral character of the gospel salvation are wrought both by Christ and by the apostles. The church, as the new Eve, shares in this aspect of the restored dominion. (2) In the gospels these saving acts of power may be said to have always a Christological significance inasmuch as they proceed from the person of the Christ and manifest his power to save.

[1] See above, par. 1 and note 1.
[2] cp. above, Ch. III, § i (last par.), and Ch. IV, § ii.
[3] Ch. IV, § ii, and cp. *Dominion*, Ch. III, § ii.
[4] For this and what follows see above, § i.

95

There is thus a further contrast between the old and the new. The redemptive signs of the old covenant foreshadowed the transforming effects of the new creation which was yet to come, whereas the redemptive signs of the gospel history signified the present reality of that new order and embodied its effects. Perhaps this may be one reason for the full return of the 'sign' language in the fourth gospel after its severe restriction in the other three. In all the gospels, however, the dominical acts of healing have a quality which may fairly be called 'sacramental' by contrast with everything that had occurred before. Let us now proceed to examine particular incidents which appear to have been treated by the evangelist in a manner corresponding to what has just been said. The story of the feeding of five thousand men with five loaves and two fishes is told by St Mark in a manner which conveys a definitely eucharistic reference.[1] This gives some indication of what the evangelist may have in mind elsewhere. For example, in the next two chapters our Lord cures a deaf mute and a blind man. In so doing he touches the affected parts of those whom he heals, using his own saliva as a sacramental means to the healing.[2]

Again, the healing of a demoniac boy after the transfiguration is reported by this evangelist in a manner which contains a twofold suggestion. The language used suggests that the incident foreshadows the death and the resurrection of the Christ, a prediction of which follows immediately.[3] But further, if a comparison is made with St Paul's teaching, the incident as described may well be thought to suggest that, as Jesus died and rose again, so too the Christian neophyte dies and rises again in baptism at the creative call of Jesus, and through union with his death and resurrection. The healed demoniac collapsed and 'became as one *dead*, so that many were saying that he had *died*. But Jesus took him by the hand and *raised* him up; and he *arose*'.[4] The four italicized words correspond to Romans 6^{2-4}, and the prediction in 9^{31} corresponds to Romans 4^{25}. The series of incidents to which we have just referred are closely connected with

[1] cp. Mk. 6^{41} with 14^{22}.

[2] 7^{32-35}, 8^{22-25}. A fuller treatment of context and biblical background is given in *Dominion*, Ch. I, § iii. Also, for the sacramental aspect see *Confirmation*, pp. 80 *f*. For what follows see the Reference Indexes in *op. cit.*

[3] cp. Mk. 9^{25-27} with 9^{31}.   [4] $9^{26, 27}$.

(1) a repetition of the eucharistic sign in the feeding of the four thousand (8⁶), (2) the refusal of a sign from heaven (8¹²), (3) the unveiling of the messianic mystery through St Peter's confession (8²⁷ *ff*) and (4) the sign given to the inner circle of three disciples on the mount of transfiguration (9² *ff*).

For St Mark all these incidents form one coherent sequence.[1] In fulfilling the old covenant Jesus restores the true order of creation; and of this he gives appropriate signs. But the meaning of the signs is manifested only to believers who become partakers in the mission of the Christ. The messages of the prophets had often received significant embodiment in their lives and actions. Only the Messiah, however, could embody the mission of Israel perfectly, fulfilling it through death and resurrection. By so doing Jesus re-created all things in himself. But he also became the head of a new order wherein transforming processes are appropriately signified and mediated through sacramental signs. For first the Christian sacraments typify prophetically the restoration of creation to its true destiny, in which there is to be realized a harmonious, worshipful response, one and yet manifold, to the beneficent will of the Creator. The sacraments, however, are more than symbolic types. They are the typically appropriate signs through which the New Man wields his dominion as the messianic priest-king. In them we see the functions of the Redeemer and of his new order coming to present fruition within the functions of the first creation.

V

The disclosure of sacramental features in gospel healings points to certain truths of the new creation, such as the unity of the Christ mystery and the integral character of salvation. The symbolism of integral salvation illustrated in sabbath healings which restore the wholeness and completeness of creation's plan. Bodily

---

[1] The sequence is clearest from 7³¹ to 9³². But the saying about 'the children's bread' in 7²⁷ suggests an eucharistic *nuance*; and the preceding section concerning Jewish washing and eating would have an ironic touch for Christian readers whose baptismal 'washing' preceded their admission to the eucharistic 'eating'. This takes us back through a Red Sea miracle (cp. 'the fourth watch of the night' in 6⁴⁸ with 'the morning watch' in Exod. 14²⁴) to the feeding of the 5,000 (6³⁰ *ff*).

healing and forgiveness of sins are here two parts of one saving event. Aspects of saving 'wholeness' as effected by the whole New Man, Jesus and his church.

The sacramental interpretation of the gospel miracles has far-reaching theological implications. In some respects this interpretation with its implications is even more prominent in St John's Gospel than in St Mark's. Perhaps the clearest example of this is the incident recorded in John 9 which elicited from St Irenaeus such a remarkable commentary.[1] As I have shewn elsewhere, the healing of the blind man there recorded suggests a 'repetition' of creation (Genesis 2[6, 7]) in every instance of Christian initiation. For the evangelists the drawing together of gospel miracles and Christian sacraments into the continuity which belongs to a single mode of divine activity is a manifestation of an even more all-embracing mystery, namely the restoration of the Creator's original plan in the new creation. This also brings us back to a further point already mentioned.[2] The sacramental characteristics of the gospel miracles correspond to the fact that the signs and wonders of the new Exodus were manifested in the mission of the apostolic church as well as in the gospel story. The powers of the New Age are one; and the new Eve is permitted to co-operate in the restored dominion of Adam.

What was effected by Jesus and his apostles in the healing miracles continued, in some sense, to be effected in the church through the sacraments. This statement requires justification, and we shall return to it presently. What is already clear, however, is the fact that in recording the miracles the evangelists make a point of emphasizing that use of material means which is an outstanding feature of all those ecclesiastical forms of ministry which have been considered to be sacramental. The two groups of signs have in fact a fundamental unity by virtue of that which they have in common; for both alike signify and effect Christ's redeeming work of grace, and so both alike are instrumental to the messianic dominion of Jesus. This sharing of the dominion corresponds to the fact that the church is in-

[1] For full details see *Revelation*, pp. 177–182.
[2] See above, § iv, par. 4 (1). It is worthy of notice that the word: 'sign' is used in OT to designate acts of the cultus which were the Hebrew counterpart of sacraments in NT; e.g. cp. Exodus 12[13], 13[9, 16].

cluded within the total mystery of the Christ. But further, the mutual assimilation of gospel and church in this particular respect emphasizes the integral character of salvation. It is natural for *us* to think of our Lord as being occupied in his work of mercy with the healing of men's bodily ills, and again to regard the sacraments as having been ordained for our spiritual health. This clean-cut distinction, however, succeeds in stating only part of the truth. It would be more in accordance with the biblical way of thinking to say that the end signified and sought in both types of sign is the salvation of the whole man.

For example, St Luke tells how our Lord healed a woman in the synagogue on the sabbath-day, declaring that it was fitting on such a day to release a daughter of Abraham from the bond in which Satan had bound her. In the light of similar sabbath teachings in the gospels every detail of the story is seen to emphasize this point of view.[1] In the physical ills of mankind Jesus saw evidence of those works of the devil which he came to destroy.[2] His healing miracles, therefore, were new creation acts restoring the original work of the six days to that completion which is signified by the sabbath (Genesis 2^{1-3}). Accordingly, at his touch on the sabbath-day the bowed woman 'was straightened up',[3] and glorified God. Moreover, the people also praised God for 'the glorious things that were being done' by Jesus, and rightly so. For he was restoring this nature of ours, distorted as it was by Satan, to that integrity for which it was originally created in the divine image (Luke 13^{10-17}). The whole of this symbolism of integral salvation is repeated in the Acts in that first apostolic miracle of healing and in the explanation of its significance offered by St Peter (Acts 3, 4).[4]

The prophet Isaiah likened sinful Israel to a sick man; the picture is set forth in the opening paragraph of his book (1^{4-6}). St John repeats the parable and develops the theme in the cure

[1] Mark $2^{23}-3^6$ and parallels bring out the connexion of the sabbath works of Jesus with his messianic claim and with his mission to 'restore' the plan of creation. See further *Dominion*, pp. 14–56.

[2] 1 John 3^8.

[3] The same author used the same expression in his report of the quotation from Amos 9 by St James in Acts 15^{16}. The crooked tent of David and the crooked humanity of Israel were 'straightened up' by that Son of David who was also the Creator of our humanity.

[4] cp. *Dominion*, Ch. I, § iv.

at the pool of Bethzatha (or Bethesda).[1] Here the clue is given by our Lord's words to the man whom he had healed: 'Behold, thou art become whole; sin no more, lest a worse thing befall thee' (John 5[14]). The words appear to carry a twofold suggestion. There is first an indication that sickness typifies sin because there is a mysterious connexion between the two forms of disorder. But secondly, 'thou art made whole' clearly refers not only to bodily health but to the entire personality. For the man was healed from sin as well as from sickness. What was outwardly a bodily healing was spiritually a release from the malady of sin. 'Sin no more' implies an act of forgiveness conveyed through the spoken words: 'arise, take up thy bed and walk.' Bodily healing and sacramental forgiveness are two aspects of one single event. There could scarcely be a more signal example of the contrast between biblical wholeness and that Greek dualism to which we moderns are heirs. Jesus restores to the whole man that soundness of being which accords with the Creator's plan.

Once more, the synoptic gospels tell how our Lord confirmed his claim to forgive the sins of a paralytic by healing the sick man. To this St Matthew adds a significant detail. The people 'feared and glorified God who gave such authority to *men*'.[2] The plural is surely deliberate. Our Lord claimed authority to co-operate with God in the restoration of the whole man. But in this mission of co-operation he included other men along with himself, a point strongly emphasized in this gospel.[3] Moreover, as we have already seen, St Luke, in the Acts, stresses the parallel between our Lord's ministry of healing and its continuation by the apostles. So also *their* works of healing were signs of the new creation; for they signified all that was being effected in 'those who were being saved'. They signified also the share granted to the new Eve in the present dominion of Christ. Integral salvation, therefore, means that the whole man is made whole by the whole New Man, the *totus Christus*, Jesus and his church. This conclusion presupposes two Hebrew idioms of

---

[1] In John 5[1-16] a possible interpretation of the symbolism shews Israel vainly resting under the five books of Moses after thirty-eight years in the wilderness (vv. 2–5; cp. Deut. 2[14]). In 9[7] the blind man is sent to wash in the nobler pool which signifies the Messiah.

[2] Matt. 9[8]; cp. Mark 2[1-11].

[3] e.g. Matt. 16[18, 19], 18[18], 28[18-20].

thought. First, the body stands for the whole man; and secondly, the whole man can represent the community. Thus, the healing of the body corporal signifies the healing of the whole man, and therefore *can* signify the renovation of the body corporate, the community of men.[1] In biblical thought, however, this renewal takes place under two conditions. (i) It is effected in and through the *ecclesia*, that holy community which stands for the whole New Man. (ii) It embraces implicitly the whole of creation, since the messianic salvation includes the restoration of Adam's dominion.

vi

In scripture redemptive signs constitute a challenge which may be accepted or refused. As such, the Johannine signs of the new Exodus are works of mercy pointing to the one 'sign spoken against' (Luke 2[34]). A sign demanded in John 2[18-22], and again in John 6[30-35], evokes in both instances a reply pointing to the Saviour's death and resurrection. This agrees with the parallel in Matt. 12[38-40] (the sign of Jonah); and Luke 11[15-30] carries implications which require a similar conclusion.

We pass on now to another stage of the argument. We have already taken note of the fact that in his application of sacramental language to the miracles of the Exodus St Paul reminds his readers that the marvellous provision of manna and water from the rock in the wilderness did not automatically secure for Israel immunity from the spiritual dangers which beset them.[2]

> They did all eat the same spiritual meat
> And did all drink the same spiritual drink. . . .
> Howbeit with most of them God was not well pleased:
> For they were overthrown in the wilderness
> (1 Corinthians 10[3-5]).

In the next chapter the same rule is applied to those who partake of the Christian sacraments. The unworthy communicant eats and drinks judgement to himself; and this is held to explain the sickness and deaths which have occurred in the Corinthian church.[3] In this respect the sacraments conform to the general

---

[1] cp. above, pars. 3 and 4 with notes.
[2] See above, § iv, par. 3.   [3] 1 Cor 11[30].

character of redemptive signs. The sign is always two-sided, because it is a vehicle of God's call. Every invitation is also a challenge which men can, if they wish, refuse. In manifesting God's love the sign makes possible man's rejection of that love.

That the sign is set both for salvation and for judgement is a doctrine which pervades the New Testament.[1] In St John's Gospel this thesis becomes dominant. Here a large part of the book is built up on a framework of seven signs which are in striking contrast to the seven plagues of the new Exodus (Revelation 15), but perhaps more closely related, in their differences, to the signs and wonders of the original Exodus from Egypt. Instead of plagues, destroying human life and sustenance, are set forth divine works of mercy which afford refreshment and healing, light and life.[2] These are presented in such a way as to confirm the fundamental thesis which, as we have already seen, is recorded by another evangelist. All the signs derive their significance from him who is set 'for the falling and rising of many in Israel and for a sign which is spoken against'.[3] Of this sign which is to be identified with Jesus himself the fourth gospel has also significant things to say, which may be profitably compared with corresponding statements of the first and third evangelists. In those two gospels the one Christological sign is 'the sign of Jonah' concerning which I wrote in a previous volume.[4]

There are two occasions mentioned in the fourth gospel on which a sign was demanded from Jesus in proof of his authority; and to each he made a significant reply concerning himself. So also the application of the Jonah sign to himself in Matthew and Luke is evoked in response to a request for a sign.[5] In these four instances there is marked diversity in the replies attributed to our Lord. Yet on all four occasions the refusal of the sign

---

[1] e.g. cp. Heb. 2[1-4].

[2] In particular we may note the following: (i) In the first plague water is turned to blood; in the 'beginning of the signs' water is turned into wine (2^{1-11}). Later, the new Moses who provides manna in the wilderness (6^{1-14}) and flesh to eat (6^{51}), offers his own blood for wine (6^{53-56}); and finally water and blood flow from the body of the new paschal lamb (19^{34}). (ii) The last two plagues, darkness and death, are replaced by the removal of a blind man's darkness (9^7) and the restoration of a dead man to life (11^{44}).

[3] cp. above, § i, par. 2.

[4] *Dominion*, Ch. V, § vi and Ch. VI, § iii.

[5] Matt. $12^{38 \, ff}$, Luke $11^{16, \, 29 \, f}$.

demanded takes fundamentally the same form, namely the offer of a more mysterious sign which is in some sense identified with the Saviour's own person. We proceed now to the examination of the Johannine incidents. In John 2[18], after a cleansing of the temple by Jesus, the Jews ask: 'What sign showest thou to us, that thou doest these things?' Our Lord's reply is enigmatic, but is understood afterwards by the disciples to refer to the coming event of Christ's resurrection from the dead. It therefore offers a close parallel to the Matthean interpretation of the Jonah sign, where a comparison is made between our Lord's descent into hell and Jonah's visit to Sheol. On both sides of the parallel the emphasis lies upon a safe return, just as in John 2 it is the 'raising' of the body-temple after three days that is the pith of the oracular utterance. The second Johannine incident is in John 6[30-35], and must now claim our attention.

After the feeding of the five thousand a crowd of people seek Jesus, and say to him: 'What sign doest thou, that we may see and believe thee?' From what follows it appears that they looked at least for the bestowal of manna in the wilderness to be repeated. Jesus, in reply, acknowledges that divinely given type, but turns their minds to its more glorious counterpart, 'the true bread from heaven.' He then speaks of 'the bread of God' which (like the manna) 'cometh down from heaven'; and when they ask for it he replies: 'I am the bread of life.' Later his words are correctly summed up in the affirmation: 'I am the bread which came down from heaven.' The discourse which follows completes the revelation by showing that this gift of himself involves first his death and then his glorification.[1] Moreover, from verse 39 onwards the believer who partakes of the gift is promised a share in the risen life. To that particular connexion we shall return later. For the present it is sufficient to note that the demand for a sign is met by a statement like that in Chapter 2 which identifies the sign with a dying and rising Saviour. Once more there is agreement in essentials with Matthew 12[38-40]. The Old Testament types in all three instances are different (Jonah, the temple, the manna). But the conclusion of all three is the same.

At first sight St Luke's treatment of the Jonah sign does not fit easily into this threefold testimony. But there are three

---

[1] John 6, verses 41, 51, 62.

relevant points which will reinforce what I have written previously on this topic.[1] (i) In Luke 11[16] mention is made of some who, 'tempting' Jesus, 'were seeking from him a sign from heaven.' To this request our Lord does not immediately make any direct reply. But the setting of the question is significant. It follows immediately on the hostile suggestion that 'he casts out demons by Beelzebub the prince of the demons' (11[15]). Here then, was a direct fulfilment of Simeon's prophecy, recorded earlier by this same evangelist.[2] The sign from heaven is sought in an atmosphere of malignant opposition against him who is already proving to be the 'sign that is spoken against'. (ii) Our Lord replies to the hostile suggestion as one who knows himself to be already victorious over the powers of darkness: 'If I by the finger of God cast out demons, then is the kingdom of God come upon you' (11[20]). It is not he who is on trial but his critics; for 'he is set for the fall and rising of many in Israel' (2[34]). Thus he turns the sign-seekers towards himself, the one completely effectual sign. (iii) The delayed reply to the sign-seekers is explicitly made in 11[29-32]; and one of its important features lies in the fact that it takes the form of a prediction about the future: 'As Jonah became a sign to the Ninevites so shall the Son of Man be to this generation.' At present he is simply the 'sign spoken against'. Jonah did not convert his shipmates, but became their scape-goat. The preacher who converted Nineveh was one who returned from the dead; and a 'greater than Jonah is here'. The fulfilment of the prediction in 11[30] began on the Day of Pentecost, as recorded in Luke's second volume.

vii

The sign of the dying and rising Saviour in his worshipping church connects the eucharist with the resurrection. A twofold relation of the material creation to human life for good or ill manifested in the Exodus story and in the new creation. The symbolism of the Johannine signs (John 6[1-21] and 11). Ezekiel 37 foreshadows the re-creation of Israel as told in the fourth gospel. The sacrificial law of creation fulfilled in Christ. Seed-sowing

---

[1] *Dominion*, pp. 159–163.
[2] Luke 2[34]; cp. above, § i, par. 2 and § vi, par. 2.

and harvest in its Pauline applications to (*a*) resurrection and (*b*) eucharist. The sacramental forms of a restored creation.

The sign to which all other signs point is that which Jesus fulfilled through his death and resurrection, and with which, in its fulfilment, the church is one. For this is also the sign of the suffering Servant in whom his many members are justified, and by whom the many nations are to be justified, the sign of him who in his rejection was like the brazen serpent, but who in his glorification is known to us as the Lamb of God. Moreover, the church also is the effectual sign of the New Jerusalem, and, as such, awaits the Day when 'the sign of the Son of Man shall be manifested in heaven' and his elect shall be gathered together.[1] Meanwhile, in this present dispensation the eye of faith can already discern the great sign in which the Messiah and his people are one, the sign which is set 'to rule over the day and over the night, and to divide the light from the darkness'. So far as men respond to the challenging rule of this sign, to that extent they become partners of Jesus in the renewal of the divine plan for creation. Thus they begin to re-enter 'the dominion of Adam', once lost, but now restored by him whose rule brings the light of eternal day.

The situation here envisaged corresponds to the vision of the city of God descending from heaven to earth and bearing within her the Lamb, that the nations may bring their glory and honour to be transformed in the flame of his sacrifice. That brings us to the final topic of this chapter. The sacrifice of the victorious Lamb is set in the midst of the worshipping church; and this ever present reality is set forth with effectual power in the Holy Eucharist.[2] It remains for us to consider in what way this, the chief sacramental sign, is related to the greatest of the historical signs, namely the resurrection of our Lord. By this means we may hope to see more clearly the connexions between 'creation' and 'worship', and thus to prepare the ground for the concluding chapter dealing with 'The Resurrection of Man'.

The story of man's creation as told in Genesis 2, comprises two stages. First, 'God formed the man from the dust of the

[1] Matt. 24[30, 31].

[2] The scene in Rev. 4, 5 corresponds to the liturgical *praxis* of the church in ancient times.

ground'; that is, he fashioned the earthly elements into the bodily shape of a man. Then, by imparting 'the breath of life', he transformed that bodily shape into a living man. There are four points to be noted here: (1) The earthly element is made instrumental to the creative action. (2) The man so formed is transformed, passing from death to life. (3) The earthly material is itself transformed in the creative action. (4) The transformation of the material at the first stage is taken up into the transformation of the man at the second stage. These four points may be summed up in two general statements: (i) The material creation here becomes instrumental to the transformation of man. (ii) The material creation is itself transformed through its inclusion in the life of the transformed man. The truth of this double relationship is abundantly confirmed in human experience. For good or for ill man is bound up with the world in which he lives. In a fallen world, however, the connexion proves to be a curse as well as a blessing. The resources of creation become instrumental to human sin, and are themselves disordered by that fact. Thus instead of supporting human life they tend to destroy it.

This twofold relationship of the material creation to the life of man, with its alternate possibilities of good or ill, is set forth in the story of the Exodus. The creaturely elements become instrumental both to the divine judgement upon Egypt and to the deliverance of Israel. But also those elements were transformed into forces, respectively destructive or beneficent, through their entry into redemptive history with its two aspects of judgement and salvation. All these factors, again, are present in the story of the new Exodus which is also the story of the new creation. For integral salvation includes the material order in its embrace, and that in two ways. The earthly elements become instrumental to the redemption of man. But also those elements are transformed through inclusion in the life of the New Man and in his redeemed order. All that has here been said might be illustrated from the sequence of seven signs in St John's Gospel, pointing forward unfailingly, as they do, to the single mystery of Christ's death and resurrection within which both the church and the sacramental order are implicitly included.

In other words the signs of the new Exodus (like the Baptist) point to the paschal Lamb, whose victory has restored creation and whose sacrifice is the substance of worship in the redeemed order. Thus in St John's account Jesus fed the five thousand when 'the passover was nigh'. Such notes of time (or place) in the fourth gospel are not inserted with a modern passion for historical accuracy, but with a characteristically ancient feeling for symbolic factors in the situation. This sign was a type, albeit only a type,[1] of the true paschal feast in which the Lamb of God, 'the living bread which came down from heaven', gives his flesh to eat. The multitude, however, sought to make him king that he might satisfy their longing for an earthly 'utopia', although there can be no such place. Jesus, on the other hand, with 'no place' for such thoughts looked forward to preparing 'a place' for the new Israel in his sacrificial body. So the people remained in Egyptian darkness, whereas Jesus brought his disciples, as by a Red Sea miracle, 'to the land whither they were going' (John 6[1-21]).[2]

The series of wonderful works which typify the transformation of Israel into a 'whole man' culminates, according to St John, in the last and greatest of the seven signs, the raising of Lazarus from the dead. This sign, like that of Jonah, manifested Israel's true destiny and foreshadowed its fulfilment in Jesus. In the tomb lay a dead body, composed of the dust to which it should again return. Yet, by the creative act of Jesus the bodily shape became once more a living man; and in that act the whole mission of the Christ was exemplified. The prophet Ezekiel had once seen Israel as a collection of disintegrated fragments upon whom the original miracle of creation must be repeated. First, the bare bones must be reunited and receive bodily shape once more; and then the divine breath must convert dead body into living man.[3] This is what Jesus did. He gathered a number of individuals together[4] and formed them to the predestined pattern of his mystical body. That was the first stage in his creative action, when the transforming process began. Then, by his own death and resurrection he imparted to

---

[1] There is a sense in which the evangelist depreciates the significance of this sign, as also of its archetype, the manna.

[2] In the synoptic parallel Matt. 14[25] says that Jesus 'came to them, walking upon the sea, in the fourth watch of the night', that is 'the morning watch' (cp. Mark 13[35]), at which time 'the Lord looked forth upon the host of the Egyptians and discomfited them' (Exod. 14[24]).

[3] Ezek. 37.

[4] Bringing them to 'the place prepared'. Here John 1[35-51] anticipates 14[2].

this new organism the divine 'breath of life', and thus raised up 'the temple of his body'.[1] As, in the first stage, the individual elements had been shaped into the body, so now that body received life, the new life of the New Man in his wholeness, Jesus and his church.

The analogy thus traced between the two creations applies not only in the historical order, but also in the sacramental. Moreover, by such twofold application the relation between these two orders can be seen to have its roots in a single plan of creation. The earthly elements which the Creator moulds into the human body do not lose their individual qualities; but they must needs forego that specific 'rhythm' which they have exhibited in another, and quite different, set of relationships. Just so, the individuals whom our Lord gathered into the organism of his body had to forego their previous way of life, conforming themselves to his new way. This change of 'rhythm' corresponds to a universal law in the pattern of creation.[2] It is a mystery of which the secret was finally laid open in the sacrifice of Christ. The essentially sacrificial character of this law is implicit in our Lord's parables of seed-sowing, and becomes explicit in the Johannine form of that figure of speech as applied to Christ's death and resurrection.[3] St Paul, who developed this comparison in detail,[4] also shows its eucharistic significance. Here the analogy takes a new form, yet the law remains the same. As the many seeds of corn are ground up by man and then kneaded into a single loaf of bread, so 'we the many are one bread, one body, for we all partake of the one bread'.[5]

But further, 'the one bread' of which we partake is that which Jesus identified with his body; and this language carries a further thought. When bread is eaten it undergoes transformation. It becomes identified with the life of a man as the material

[1] cp. *Confirmation*, pp. 176 f and notes.

[2] As I have indicated in *The Incarnate Lord* (1928, Longmans).

[3] John 12[24].

[4] Connecting it with Gen. 1, 2, and finding the culminating point in Gen. 2[7] (1 Cor. 15[35-49]; cp. 15[20 ff]).

[5] 1 Cor. 10[17]. The connexion between these two forms of the seed analogy was, perhaps, not consciously present in St Paul's mind. Yet he had already identified the new Israel with the unleavened bread of the new passover (5[6-8]). Moreover, in 15[20, 23] he identifies Jesus with 'the sheaf of the first-fruits' (Lev. 23[9-11]), which was offered in the temple on the first Easter-Day, as appears by comparing Acts 2[1] with Lev. 23[15 ff].

of his body. In the miracle of the loaves and fishes this law was enhanced; for the food was transformed in respect of its capacity to satisfy those who ate. In the new passover, however, the bread is transformed because it is there identified with the Lamb of God as the material of his eucharistic body. Thus it surpasses all other food in power to satisfy. At this point we can see the fundamental distinction between baptism and the eucharist. In the former the earthly element is instrumental to the transformation of man; in the latter the earthly elements are themselves transformed. By ritual use of water the mystery of Christ's death and resurrection is re-enacted in the individual neophyte through his identification with Christ's sacrifice. By ritual consecration of bread and wine, on the other hand, those earthly elements are themselves identified with Christ's sacrifice; and thus the mystery of Christ's death and resurrection is re-enacted in the midst of the worshipping community.[1]

Both sacraments, then, effect the reversal of that disorder which ensued when the resources of creation were made instrumental to sin. In the sacramental order, however, it is the eucharist which is specifically the effectual sign of Adam's dominion restored in Christ, the true priest-king of this creation. For here the creaturely gifts of God to his human family are offered to the Father by redeemed mankind in that one acceptable sacrifice with which they are identified. Thus, both the creaturely gifts and the community through which they are offered are gathered up and unified in the lowly response of the Son, in whom they together return to the site of their creation.

Additional Note A.

The Words of Christ

This note is concerned solely with our Lord's words concerning the bread and wine in his institution of the eucharist at the Last Supper, in so far as Hebrew idioms of thought may be held to throw fresh light upon the subject. In scripture the word of God is creative; and in Chapter III of the present volume certain aspects of that creativity have been examined in detail. But it appears also that in the Hebrew way of thinking human words may under some circum-

---

[1] For fuller explanation of 're-enacted' see *Revelation*, Ch. IX, § iv, last par., pp. 280*f*.

stances have remarkable potency. In the story which tells how Jacob obtained from his father the parental blessing intended for his brother (Genesis 27) there is implicit an assumption that words of blessing inevitably take effect upon the person to whom they are addressed, and that even where there has been a mistake of identity this effect is irreversible. Further, wherever the speaker is a genuine representative of the deity it appears that the divine word takes effect through a human voice. So it was with Moses and the prophets. A classic statement of what happens when the divine word is so uttered is to be found in Isaiah 55[10, 11]. Here the word passes from the divine mouth through the mouth of the human agent, charged with unfailing potency to achieve the Creator's purpose. As I have pointed out elsewhere, this certainty of fulfilment is conceived to have its parallel in the unchanging routine of nature as described in verse 10 (cp. *Revelation*, p. 231).

In Matthew 24[35] Jesus is reported to have said: 'Heaven and earth shall pass away, but my words shall not pass away'; and this utterance, in turn, corresponds to the teaching of the Johannine prologue. Jesus is the Creator-Word incarnate. He is not a human agent of the divine word; for he is that Word in its fulness, possessing all its creative power. In his incarnate life on earth he spoke human words, words which, nevertheless, had in them all the creative power and sovereign authority of God the Son, the author of both creations. So when he took bread and said 'This is my body' he creatively identified the bread with his body. No other conclusion is consistent with the biblical way of thinking, that way of thinking which, in turn, provides the essential form wherein revelation has been given. Only one thing more needs to be said. The words of Christ 'shall not pass away'. So when those words concerning the bread and the wine are repeated in a duly authorized way the incarnate Word acts through his human representative, and the creative identification takes place. In the solemn repetition of the apostolic tradition concerning this matter which St Paul makes in 1 Corinthians 11[23 *ff*] his severe warning concerning any unworthy partaking of the eucharistic elements implies that such conduct is a sacrilegious treatment of Christ's body and blood. The conclusions reached in this note must be set upon the wider background of theological unities briefly indicated in the paragraphs which immediately precede and follow.

CHAPTER V

THE RESURRECTION OF MAN

i

The sacraments within the total Christ mystery of the transfigured life. The consummation of creation in the sacrifice of Calvary set forth before God and man in the eucharist by Jesus in his church. The sacrificial 'ascent' of Jesus and his people wherein the earthly elements of this creation are taken up and transformed. The eucharistic transformation shows forth this greater mystery. The cosmic range of the sacramental order corresponds to the scriptural imagery of new creation.

The tendency of the evangelists to refer back the sacramental order of the church into the gospel narratives points to the conclusion that what was said earlier about the church is true also of the sacraments. They also may be regarded as being included along with the church in the single mystery of Christ's death and resurrection wherein the dominion of Adam is restored. For they are the appointed means through which the life of the church is conformed to that mystery as it was foreshadowed upon the mount of transfiguration. If, however, the members of Christ are being in such wise transfigured in the church, this fact, in turn, depends upon the more fundamental truth that the transfigured Christ is still present to his disciples in the church as once upon the mount. According to St Luke (9[31, 34]) Moses and Elias 'appeared in glory' and the apostolic witnesses entered into the overshadowing cloud. St Paul takes us further in his contrast between the two covenants, when he says that 'we all, with unveiled face beholding as in a mirror[1] the glory of the Lord, are transformed into the same image from glory to glory'.[2] Moses' face shone for a while, because he was admitted to the secret place where the divine glory is unveiled.

[1] Or 'reflecting as a mirror'. Possibly both meanings are intended.
[2] 2 Cor. 3[18]; cp. 4[6, 7].

In the new covenant, however, the sacrifice of the victorious Lamb is set in the midst of the worshipping church; and this ever-present reality is set forth with effectual power in the Holy Eucharist. That is for us pre-eminently the place where the glory is unveiled.

We have now reached a point where we may, perhaps, articulate more precisely earlier statements to the effect that the church represents and embodies Christ, as setting forth his obedience to the Father before God and man.[1] This function of the church is, of course, signified by the very fact of her existence. It receives, however, its formal and ritual fulfilment in the sacrificial aspect of the eucharist.[2] There the identification of bread and wine with Christ's body and blood signifies the true goal of creation. God made all things, and saw that they were good. For he made all things in his Son, that is, in the pre-destined Lamb of God. All things, therefore, are stamped with a sacrificial character which they derive from the very source and site of their creation. Their destiny can thus be fulfilled only in a community of sacrificial interchange in which every created element and every creature is involved, however diversely. When the Word became flesh the foundations of this cosmic temple of sacrifice were re-established. Then the altar of this created world was once more set upon its base, and the flame was once more lighted for the sacrifice which was consummated upon Calvary.[3]

The eucharistic memorial signifies the taking up of all creaturely things through consecration into union with Christ's sacrifice so consummated; and through the words and actions of the celebrant the church participates in this high-priestly action of her Saviour. Accordingly, the return of God's creaturely gifts to their Creator, in harmony with his preordained plan, and in response to his call, is effected on behalf of all men through the worshipful obedience of the whole New Man, the dedicated Servant of the Lord, Jesus in his church. Now in the very act of 'setting forth' before God the obedience of the Christ to the Father the church also, although in another sense, sets forth that same obedience before man. The eucharistic identifi-

---

[1] e.g. Ch. I, end of § v.

[2] For what follows the reader is referred back to the last three pars. of Ch. IV with the Additional Note.

[3] For OT background see further next note.

cation of the church with the risen Lord in his high-priestly
action manifests or 'proclaims' to mankind the fact of the
Saviour's death in its redemptive power and in its cosmic signi-
cance. Thus the descending city of God brings the divine victim
down upon his saving, and yet also challenging, mission to the
peoples of the world, that they, in turn, may bring their share of
creation's treasures to the place of sacrifice.

Here we return to the parallel between the holy city 'descending out of heaven' and the Lamb of God who 'came down
out of heaven' to die, in order that thereafter he might 'go up'
or 'ascend' to the Father. This language is characteristic of St
John's Gospel and may have a double meaning. For Hebrew
idiom referred to a sacrifice as 'going up' or 'ascending' to God.
Our Lord came down out of heaven in order that he might go
up to the Father as a sacrifice whose savour is acceptable.[1] So
also the holy city descends from heaven that through its open
gates the peoples may 'ascend' bringing their glory and honour
to deck the sacrifice of the Lamb. But again, there is contrast.
The Son of God entered his creation in order that the whole
created order might provide material of his sacrifice, and might
thus be transformed in him. This took place once for all in his
death and resurrection. For, through their identity with the
mortal flesh which once hung upon the cross, the earthly elements of this creation were taken up and transformed in that
same flesh of Jesus when it was raised from the tomb. Moreover,
it is this mystery which is continuously being renewed in the life
of the church in and through the sacramental order.

But further, the transformation of earthly elements into
Christ's body and blood by repeated acts of eucharistic consecration is the sacramental memorial of a yet greater trans-

[1] See Gen. 8[20, 21], where the ascending flame and smoke penetrates to
the throne of deity as a 'sweet savour' (cp. Eph. 5[2] and 2 Cor. 2[15, 16]). In
John the crucial passage is 7[1-14]. In 1 Kings 18[29, 36] the 'going up' of the
(evening) sacrifice is mentioned; and in 18[29] the LXX rendering ('the time
of the going up') provides a verbal background to the well-authenticated
reading in John 7[8]: 'I go not up unto this feast, for my time is not yet fulfilled.' Jesus goes up to the heavenly feast by a sacrificial ascent. Like Elijah
he rebuilds the altar; and, as then on Carmel so now, his action must be
consummated at the appointed 'time of the going up of the sacrifice'. Elsewhere in this gospel the language of 'ascent' has a sacrificial context, as in
6[62], following vv. 48–58, and again in 20[17], where it immediately precedes
the showing of the wounds.

I   113

formation. For the eucharist proclaims that one death which is the gate of life to all, inasmuch as he who died that death also rose again. The range of the sacramental order in the church is thus seen to extend backwards and forwards so that it reaches both to the beginning and to the end of the divine plan. Its range, indeed, is that of the whole new creation, which takes up the first creation into itself and brings it at length to its final consummation in him who is both the Alpha and the Omega, the beginning and the end. At this point, however, it will be well to recall the fact that the biblical form of 'new creation' imagery corresponds closely to that of the creation stories in Genesis. Thus the comprehensive scope of the sacramental order corresponds to the far-reaching functions of the new Eve, that is, the Israel of God regarded as the human agent through whom the obedience of the new Adam is to become effectual in all. The bearing of this topic upon the main theme of the present chapter must be reserved to a new section.

ii

The visions in Rev. 12 and 21 show cross-connexions; and together they span the whole story of redemption. Two aspects of the resurrection in NT, both for the Christ and for his members. A fresh act of God, and yet also a transformation of the old in the new. Apostolic agreement concerning new creation imagery as background to the hope of resurrection. The argument of 1 Cor. 15^{35-49} shows detailed analogy and connexion between the two creations.

In the Revelation of St John two quite distinct visions are recorded, each of which, however, might be said to be concerned with the figure of 'the new Eve'. The pictures set forth respectively in Chapters 12 and 21 correspond, as we have seen, to the double truth that Jesus is both the promised seed of the woman and the bridegroom of the church. In both aspects, however, he is the new Adam; and both visions contain suggestions that the part of Israel, as the new Eve, is correspondingly one. Thus, in the earlier vision the Christian martyrs are children of Emmanuel's mother,[1] and in the later vision the

---

[1] 'The rest of her seed' (12^{17}).

Lamb is carried within the holy city, his bride, as a child is carried by its mother. Moreover, when the two visions are thus brought together they show in outline the whole course of redemption. For whereas the former vision traces the new order back to its divine origin by showing the entry of the new into the old, the vision of the descending city anticipates the end by showing the entry of the old order into the new, as the peoples go up into the city. In Chapter 12 the great conflict is inaugurated; in Chapter 21 it is already concluded. The leaven entered the lump, and thereby set going a disturbance which will issue in final transformation.

When 'the whole is leavened' integral salvation will be consummated in the general resurrection. Concerning this the Christian apocalypse has two quite distinct ways of speaking, to which we shall return later.[1] At present, by way of preface, two observations may be made about the teaching of the New Testament as a whole. In the first place the resurrection of man is no mere supplement or corollary of redemption. It is of one texture with the whole pattern of the new creation in Christ; and only when so regarded can it be rightly understood. On the other hand, the resurrection is not an inevitable result of what precedes, but rather a gracious act of God which only he can bring about. It follows, then, that the resurrection must be characterized both by continuity and by discontinuity with what comes before it in the order of redemption. Moreover, in this respect the harvest will be like the firstfruits.[2] Between the death of Jesus and his resurrection there was discontinuity. Death was the end of this mortal life; and the sacred body was raised by a new creative act of God. There was a divine entry of the new into human history like that which took place when the same body was formed in the virginal conception.

Yet, on the other hand, the wounds in the risen body shewed the continuity of the new with the old. So, too, the consummation for which we look is not the replacement of this earthly life by some other world wholly discontinuous with what went before it. The resurrection will be the ingathering of a harvest, long since sown and now finally ripened. It will involve, therefore, a radical transfiguration of this earthly life by its Creator in such wise that all its treasures are taken up into a splendour

---

[1] See *Additional Note B*.   [2] I Cor. 15[20-23].

of uncreated glory which can never pass away. Thus the victorious issue of the new creation is vitally connected with its heavenly origin; and the hope of the resurrection has the same foundation. For St Paul Jesus is the seed, not of the earth-born Adam, but 'of a woman'; and the second Adam, unlike the first is 'from heaven'.[1] In him, therefore, we shall be quickened; and when that life-giving transformation takes place we shall exchange the image characteristic of our earthly origin for the image of the heavenly Adam to whom we are now united.[2] Moreover, as we trace our present corruptible and mortal bodies to one who came from the dust and returned to the dust, so also we shall receive incorruptible and immortal bodies corresponding to our quickening in the risen Christ.[3]

Here St John the divine supplements St Paul. Since we are in Christ we are children, not of Adam, but of the new Eve. We therefore share in the triumph of Emmanuel who entered this creation to be enthroned as its ruling power.[4] Similarly St Paul's teaching about the resurrection is closely connected with the narratives of the first creation. All the great creaturely divisions mentioned in 1 Corinthians 15 appear also in Genesis 1. The apostle, however, makes two changes of order. In his version the sequence of living organisms is reversed and becomes a descending scale. This change has the effect of bringing man next to the seed sown in the ground with which the body of the resurrection is being compared (verses 35–39). Secondly, in Genesis the heavenly bodies come after the plants. St Paul, on the other hand, mentions them last of all. In so doing he places them above earthly bodies, and emphasizes the contrast between these two groups:

There are also celestial bodies and bodies terrestrial; but the glory of the celestial is one, and the glory of the terrestrial is another.

Lastly there follows a third descending scale consisting of sun, moon and stars. The contrast here between earthly and heavenly bodies prepares the way for the difference between the 'natural' and the spiritual body and, finally, between the man who came from the earth and the man who came from heaven.[5]

[1] cp. 1 Cor. 15⁴⁷ and Gal. 4⁴ with Gen. 2⁷ and 3¹⁵.
[2] 1 Cor. 15²², ⁴⁷⁻⁴⁹, Rom. 8²⁹.
[3] Gen. 3¹⁹; 1 Cor. 15⁴⁸ and 15⁵⁰⁻⁵⁷.
[4] Rev. 12¹⁻⁵, ¹⁰, ¹¹, ¹⁷.   [5] With 1 Cor. 15⁴¹⁻⁴⁴ cp. Dan. 12², ³.

Thus the apostle brings before us in succession five orders of being, charting heaven and earth in the two realms of creation, old and new:

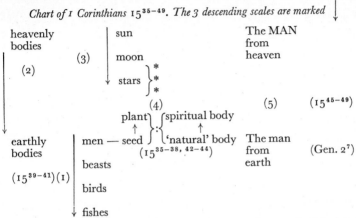

Chart of 1 Corinthians 15^{35-49}. The 3 descending scales are marked

(1) to (3) are inserted, in that order, into the analogy set forth in (4) in order to illustrate the differences of grade implied in the analogy. But (2) also provides an analogue for the contrast in (5) upon which the whole argument turns, as indicated in 15^{20-28}.
With 1 Cor. 15^{24-28} cp. Genesis 1^{28}.
With 1 Cor. 15^{36-39} cp. Genesis $1^{29, 30}$.

The conclusion of this whole series shows 'the Man from heaven' occupying the ruling position in the second creation corresponding to that which was assigned to the sun in the first creation. That, again, fits perfectly with the imagery which we have already examined in Revelation 12^1. Yet once more the later picture supplements the earlier. For in the seer's vision Emmanuel 'was caught up to God and to his throne', that is, to a position *above* the heavenly bodies. Thus the restored dominion of Adam was finally secured. This conclusion is, in fact, implicit in an earlier section of the great chapter on the resurrection (verses 24–28); and for the thought implied in Revelation 12^5 we may compare other statements in the Pauline *corpus*.[1]

iii

The two aspects of the resurrection in 1 Cor. 15 and 2 Cor. 5. The body-garment and the body-building. The biblical back-

[1] e.g. Phil. 2^{9-11} and Eph. 4^{10}.

ground to 2 Cor. 5[1] provides an Israelite frame for three stages of
the new creation in Christ. Bodily identity between Christ and
his apostle unfolded under three images: the lamp, the sacrificial
victim and the sanctuary (2 Cor. 4[4]-5[1]). Finally, the new body-
sanctuary is announced as already in being, and that too in language reflecting a significant gospel tradition.

St Paul concludes as he began with the contrast between the
two Adams, a contrast upon which depends the distinction between the firstfruits and the harvest. We belong to Christ; for
we are risen with him. Yet the effects of our former relation to
the first Adam are not yet done away. So the final transformation in us must await the general resurrection. What, then, is
the relation between our present mortal body and the body of
the resurrection? This is the crucial question which we must
now begin to consider. In the argument which we have been
examining two complementary truths appear to be asserted.
The analogy of the seed sown in the ground and then springing
up in plant form suggests continuity: 'That which thou sowest
is not quickened except it die.' Does this imply that the mortal
body is transformed into the risen body? It would, perhaps, be
more accurate to say that the person who died is transformed in
the resurrection. This corresponds to the analogy. For the outer
husk of the seed decays; but the interior germ of life continues
and receives new form. So the analogy also suggests discontinuity: 'That which thou sowest, thou sowest not the body
which shall come into being . . . but God giveth to it a body.'[1]

In the later stages of the apostle's argument a new form of
analogy emerges, to which we must now give attention. In verse
50 discontinuity is stressed in the statement that 'flesh and blood
cannot inherit the kingdom of God, neither doth corruption
inherit incorruption'. What follows, however, makes it clear that
a transformation is to take place in which the state of mortality
will be transcended. 'The dead shall be raised incorruptible';
and those who survive until the Lord's return 'will be changed'.
At this point a new form of imagery is introduced: 'For this
corruptible must put on incorruption and this mortal must put
on immortality.' It appears probable that this statement refers
primarily to the second group, those who have not died; and

---

[1] 1 Cor. 15[36-38].

the expression: 'put on' introduces the new analogy. As a garment can be put on over other clothes, so the body of the resurrection will be put on over the mortal body. Since, however,
mortal and corruptible flesh cannot 'enter the kingdom' the new
garment will effect the necessary change. Death will be victoriously and finally 'swallowed up', that is, destroyed. The mortal
body will thus be transformed by assimilation to its more glorious covering.[1]

In the opening paragraph of 2 Corinthians 5 the clothing
analogy appears again.[2] Once more we are told that Christians
who do not die before the second coming of Christ will be
'clothed upon' with the new body of the resurrection; the old
will be transformed in the new. Moreover, both passages emphasize a contrast between the earthly and the heavenly; yet the
differences are also striking. In particular a contrast is made in
2 Corinthians between two kinds of building. Our present
mortal body is called 'our earthly tent-house', whereas the body
of the resurrection is described as 'a house not made with hands
eternal in the heavens'. This contrast between a tent and a
house recalls to mind the teaching of St John's Gospel concerning the fleshly tabernacle or tent which our Lord took for his
earthly dwelling-place and, again, the permanent temple of the
risen body into which that fleshly tent was transformed on 'the
third day'.[3] The imagery here is complex because the body-
building is also a body-garment as in the former epistle. Yet that
particular combination is already present in the Old Testament
where human bodies are called 'houses of clay' and death is
described as the plucking up of a tent-cord.[4] Moreover, in the
same book Job says: 'Thou hast clothed me with skin and flesh.'[5]

The contrast between an 'earthly tent-house' and a heavenly
temple has its biblical background in the story of Israel. The
tabernacle belonged to the wilderness wanderings, whereas the
temple upon Mount Zion was associated with the triumphs of
David and the splendours of Solomon's reign. Moreover, in the
New Testament this contrast has its counterpart, not only in the

---

[1] 15[50-54]. The final clause of v. 54 is a rendering of Isa. 25[8a].

[2] And in 2 Cor. 5[4] an echo of the quotation from Isa. 25[8] recurs; see last
note.

[3] John 1[14] and 2[19-22]. Cp. *Dominion*, Ch. V, § i.

[4] Job 4[19-21].   [5] *ib.* 10[11].

Johannine version of the gospel story mentioned above, but also in the tension between the present pilgrimage of the church on earth and the heavenly glory of the New Jerusalem to which we already belong.[1] Thus the contrast between two epochs of Israel's history provides a single frame within which three stages of the new creation in Christ can be contemplated; and the connecting links of the three stages can be clearly seen in the immediate context of the passage in 2 Corinthians which we have been considering. The peculiar form of the statement concerning the mortal body and the risen body in Chapter 5 provides the culmination of an argument concerning Christ and the church in Chapters 3 and 4. But here it must be pointed out that, as in the Old Testament so also in the New, the Israelite frame of reference is set within the yet wider context of creation. We must, then, attempt to trace these inter-connexions in the apostle's detailed exposition.

In Chapters 3 and 4 the glory to which we have access in the face of Jesus the Christ is contrasted with the transient glory which appeared for a while upon the face of Moses in the wilderness. On the other hand in 4^{4-6} it is connected with the glory with which man was crowned[2] by virtue of the image of God in which he was created. Christ *is* that image, and as such he is the source of both creations. As then in the beginning God said 'let there be light' so now he has 'shined in our hearts to give the light of the knowledge of the glory of God in the face of Jesus Christ'. Each of the three images which follow this sentence is presented to us as receiving its fulfilment in the apostle through his identity with the Christ. The treasure which 'we have in earthen vessels' (4^7) is the light of revelation streaming from the face of Jesus. It may be thought of therefore as a bright flame burning in an earthen lamp. The humble lamp bears aloft the precious light of the glory with which the second Adam was crowned. But further, the light of revelation in Jesus illuminates precisely because it is in essence sacrificial. So in the next image the mortal flesh of the apostle is seen to be the body of a sacrificial victim which is 'being delivered up for Jesus' sake' to the death of the suffering Servant (4^{10-12}). Finally, when its mortal frailty and earthly origin are considered, that same body is seen to be like the tabernacle journeying through the wilderness. As

[1] cp. above Ch. I, § viii and Ch. II, § iv. [2] Ps. 8^5.

such it already contains the Shekinah glory; yet it is destined at last to be taken down, and to be replaced by a permanent sanctuary which is already being prepared in the heavenly Zion.

The more permanent body-building which is to replace the 'tent-house' is described by the apostle as 'a house made without hands' which 'we have in process of building[1] from God' (5[1]). Now at his trial before the high-priest Jesus was charged with having said: 'I will destroy this temple made with hands, and in three days I will build another made without hands.' St Mark, here quoted (14[58]), appears to have preserved the accusation in its full form. More briefly it is repeated by mocking bystanders at Calvary (15[29]);[2] and it seems to be echoed in the charge brought against St Stephen (Acts 6[14]). Finally the fourth evangelist records what he clearly holds to be the original words of Jesus upon which the charge was based (John 2[19]). There is an obvious affinity of language between the phraseology of the statement in 2 Corinthians 5[1] and the words attributed to our Lord in St Mark's account.[3] There is, therefore, good ground for thinking that in those words a genuine utterance of Jesus is echoed. From all this two conclusions emerge. The apostle speaks of his own resurrection body as already coming into existence, and he describes it in terms which may probably be traced to a saying of the Christ concerning *his* own resurrection body. The full significance of these conclusions must next be considered.

iv

The key to the two aspects of apostilic teaching concerning the resurrection to be found in (1) the corresponding mystery of identity and distinction between Christ and the church and (2) the analogy of the transfiguration foreshadowing final glory. The gulf between present mortality and the risen body bridged by an interior process of transformation. St Paul's conviction that death

---

[1] For this rendering see J. A. Robinson, Comm. on Eph. 2[21], pp. 70 *f* and 164.*f.*

[2] As also in the Matthean version on both occasions (26[61], 27[40]).

[3] To 'building' in 2 Cor. 5[1] corresponds the verb ('I will build') in Mark; cp. also John 2[20]. The word which we render 'dissolved' in 2 Cor. 5[1] also occurs in both the synoptic records.

may come before Christ's return in tension with the conviction
that the 'earnest' of the Spirit anticipates the final 'redemption
of the body'.

In the last section reference was made to three stages of the
new creation in Christ with connecting links. The three stages
are represented by Christ, the church and the general resurrection. The connecting links were seen as they were exhibited in
the body of the apostle. This personal application provides a
graphic illustration of the unity and continuity which characterizes the Christ mystery as a whole. We have now reached a
point where it becomes clear that the oneness or 'one flesh' of
Christ and the church is the key to the teaching of scripture
concerning our hope of resurrection and concerning the relation
between our present condition and our final destiny. The two
aspects of the resurrection doctrine, continuity and discontinuity, correspond to the two aspects which we have previously
noted in the present situation of the visible church on earth.
Moreover there, as here, what I have called 'the Israelite frame
of reference' provides the contrasted images of lowliness and
glory, of present pilgrimage and ultimate security, which characterize the Israel of God as a whole. Here, however, we must
take note of a factor which confronted us quite early in this
volume, and which has an intimate bearing upon the theme of
this present chapter.

The factor to which I have just referred is indicated in
Chapter I above, where in the summary prefixed to section v it
was stated that 'in the mystery of Christ and the church the
Whole transcends its historical sequence, so that every event in
the new creation has the significance of the whole'; and *yet* 'the
sequence is cumulative'. So the church on earth is in a lowly
state of pilgrimage looking forward to a final state of glory; and
yet there is a sense in which we are already present in the New
Jerusalem, 'seated in the heavenly places in Christ' (Ephesians
2⁶). This combination of simultaneity and sequence corresponds
once more to all that has been said in the present volume concerning the significance of our Lord's transfiguration as re-
enacted in the church 'with a significantly detailed parallelism,
e.g. a foreshadowing of final glory in our present mortal flesh'.[1]

---

[1] Ch. I. Summary to § vii.

It seems that this foreshadowing of final glory can secure a genuine continuity between our present mortal flesh and that body of the resurrection which for *our* present consciousness belongs to a distant future.[1] So the apostle affirms that we already 'have' it in the heavenly order of being.

In the light of these considerations we can now begin to see how the arguments of the two Corinthian epistles take us to the very heart of the Christian doctrine of the resurrection. In the second epistle the argument depends upon the identification of the apostle's body with that flesh of Jesus which has already been transformed into the risen body. We are risen with Christ; but his dying and rising together form one mystery. So by daily dying with him we continue to partake of his risen life. This mystical identification bridges the gulf which lies between our present mortality and the full glory of the resurrection, and again between earth and heaven. The sanctuary of the heavenly Zion is not a distant place or a future event, but a present reality to which the earthly tabernacle is mysteriously united. The hidden transformation now taking place in the mortal body has identity with that building-process by which the temple of Christ's body is being raised for all of us in the New Jerusalem. For our mortal bodies are already members of his risen body.[2] Thus the hidden process is already preparing us for that final transformation when we shall be 'clothed upon' with the bright garment of the risen life.

Before we carry further this analysis of apostolic teaching it is desirable that we should take note of an important change of outlook which has supervened since the earliest period of church history. The first Christians expected our Lord's second advent to occur during their own life-time. Much of St Paul's own teaching appears to be dominated by this outlook, certainly in his earlier epistles. Consequently the gap between the earthly life and the general resurrection would not seem to them so serious or so formidable as it may well do for us. Yet in 2 Corinthians 5[1–10], the passage we have been considering, the apostle is evidently facing the possibility that he may die before the Lord's return. Already he is beginning to labour under a physical strain (verse 4); yet he seems to be daunted by the thought of dying (being 'unclothed'), when he would fain be 'clothed

---

[1] See next par. but one.   [2] I Cor. 6[14, 15].

upon' with the garment of the resurrection without the grim disembodiment which death involves. Death would then be 'swallowed up by life'. There is a similar passage in Philippians 1^{19–24}, and the change of tone in the later utterance is not without significance, as we shall see later.

In both contexts there is a reference to the Holy Spirit which is more amply clarified by the much fuller statement in an intermediate epistle (Romans 8). The three epistles together set before us the various stages of that hidden process which is to issue in the final transformation. In Romans 6 we are taken back to the starting point when, in baptism, we died with Christ and began to partake of his risen life. So also in 2 Corinthians 5⁵ the apostle connects the body of the resurrection, the heavenly garment in which he is to be clothed, with the God-given 'earnest' or firstfruit of the Spirit which is the complement of baptism. Earlier in this same epistle he had already described this 'baptismal' gift of the Spirit in terms of 'anointing' and 'sealing' (1^{21, 22}).[1] As members of the Christ, that is the Lord's anointed one, we partake in the endowment of the Spirit with which he was anointed. This constitutes a vital bond between the earthly tabernacle and the heavenly temple. For those who belong to the Christ share his victorious entry into the heavenly Zion by which Adam's dominion is restored.[2]

Accordingly, whilst they still bear in their earthly body the image of the man who was formed from the dust of the ground, yet that body, like the tabernacle in the wilderness, is overshadowed by the cloud of the divine presence. It has received the indwelling Spirit from him who is 'life-giving Spirit'. This fact is the pledge that, through 'the redemption of our body' we shall one day 'bear the image of the heavenly'.[3] In Romans 8¹¹ the matter is succinctly summed up:

> If the Spirit of him that raised up Jesus from the dead dwelleth in you, he that raised up Christ Jesus from the dead shall quicken also your mortal bodies through his Spirit that dwelleth in you.

It will be noticed that in this statement continuity is markedly stressed by the language about quickening the mortal body, and

---

[1] The gift is 'baptismal' in the biblical way of speaking, because all the stages of Christian initiation belong to the one baptismal mystery, as I have explained in *Confirmation*.

[2] 1 Cor. 15^{22–28}.   [3] 1 Cor. 15^{45–49}, Rom. 8^{23, 29}.

this emphasis is repeated later in Philippians 3^{21}, where it is in obvious contrast to the earlier statement in the same epistle to which we have already drawn attention in the present section. This remarkable fluctuation demands an explanation, which we shall undertake later in this chapter. But first we must complete our survey of the apostolic teaching as a whole.

V

The redemption of creation, implicit in 1 Cor. 15, is in Rom. 8 explicitly related to the redemption of the body. The categories in 1 Cor. 15^{36} ^{ff} ('seed' and 'flesh', 'earthly' and 'heavenly') lead on naturally to the parallels in Rom. 4–8 between physical birth and (a) the resurrection of Jesus, (b) the hidden process of spiritual re-birth issuing in resurrection, (c) a cosmic re-birth of all creation. Gen. 3 as background of Rom. 8$^{19-23,\ 29}$ (and possibly 2 Cor. 5$^{2-4}$).

In the Epistle to the Romans St Paul sums up his doctrine of the resurrection in a way which shows its relation on the one hand to the new life in Christ and on the other hand to the redemption of creation as a whole. Salvation is integral; and therefore the inward process set up by mystical union with Christ must issue in an outward transformation which has universal effects. Conversely the destiny of creation waits upon the redemption of man, its true head. This, in turn, can be completed only through the re-integration of 'body' and 'spirit' (8$^{9-11}$) into that wholeness in which the image of God's Son is perfectly restored.[1] The introduction of the creationist theme in Romans 8^{19} ^{ff} adds a third factor to the duality of body and spirit; and this threefold presentation corresponds broadly to the analogy from nature developed in 1 Corinthians 15. For there we find three ideas embodied in a single illustration, namely: (1) a hidden process of change which (2) is crowned by a God-given embodiment, so that (3) the outward structure of nature is thereby transformed. It will be worth while, then, at this point to see whether interconnexions of thought as between a group of Pauline epistles can throw fresh light upon the move-

[1] Rom. 8$^{9-30}$.

ment of the apostle's mind concerning the subject which we are investigating.

In 1 Corinthians 15 the *primâ facie* scope of the analogy is a comparison between the transformation of the seed sown in the ground and a corresponding transformation of the body laid in the tomb.[1] But the sentences which follow indicate that there are many such analogies in nature, and that they are not all of the same type. The transition from various kinds of 'seed' to various kinds of 'flesh' inevitably suggests the parallel which the apostle actually drew in Romans between the mystery of human birth and the miracle of the resurrection.[2] In fact the catalogue of bodies earthly and heavenly, which leads to the contrast between the 'natural' and the spiritual, might also suggest the analogy between physical birth on the one hand and spiritual rebirth 'from heaven' on the other.[3] For in both of these there is involved a hidden process. Moreover, the fact that the hidden process of physical birth issues in a marvellously new embodiment of life might serve to connect the hidden process of spiritual re-birth with a divinely given re-embodiment of life. It might serve, in short, to connect the mystical dying and rising with Christ in the sacrament of baptism with a sure and certain hope that after physical death our bodies will be raised at the last day. Thus it would appear that the thought of the apostle upon this theme underwent a natural development.

The sequence of ideas which we have found pictorially presented in the two Corinthian epistles recurs in yet other forms in Romans. Here we have first the analogy between Isaac wonderfully born of aged parents and Jesus unexpectedly fulfilling the Servant prophecy in his death, burial and resurrection. The transformed status of those whom the Servant justifies is then developed by means of the contrast between the two Adams, the

[1] This follows from the question in verse 35; and it also agrees with a corresponding parallel in Isa. 26¹⁹.

[2] Rom. 4¹⁷⁻²⁵. For 'seed' and 'flesh' see Gen. 7², ³. It may well be that in 1 Cor. 15³⁶ *ff* St Paul has in mind our Lord's parable of the mustard seed, identifying the latter with Christ, 'the seed' of Abraham. With 'a grain of mustard seed' (Mark 4³¹, Matt. 17²⁰) cp. the 'bare grain' of 1 Cor. 15³⁷. Our Lord stripped himself bare and naked in death. But through his nakedness we are clothed with heavenly garments, as God is said to have clothed the nakedness of Adam and Eve (Gen. 3²¹).

[3] This analogy is implicit in John 3, as appears from the question of Nicodemus in verse 4.

earthly and the heavenly. Finally the analogy between Isaac and the true 'seed' of Abraham is transcended. For our spiritual re-birth in baptism is not merely compared, but mystically identified with the death, burial and resurrection of the Christ.[1] Along these lines the argument of Romans 4^{17}–6^{14} combines the teachings of 1 Corinthians 15^{1-49} and 2 Corinthians 4^{6-14}, 5^{14-17} with that of Galatians 3^{16-29}. Through baptism we are identified with the promised 'seed' of Abraham in the transforming process of death and resurrection which that 'seed' underwent. Thus we return to Romans 8 which shows the inward process issuing in outward transformation with universal effects.

Here once more, and now in the most far-reaching fashion, the mystery of birth is connected with the miracle of resurrection. When baptismal re-birth through union with Christ in his death and resurrection is crowned at last with the God-given embodiment of the risen life through 'the redemption of our body', then, and not till then, will the travail of creation itself be brought to its consummation in the re-birth of the world.[2] The biblical background of this section is the story of man's fall and its consequences as set forth in Genesis 3. There a fourfold curse is pronounced: first, upon the serpent whose head is to be bruised by the seed of the woman; secondly, upon the woman who will bring forth children in sorrow. Thirdly the curse is pronounced upon the ground from which thorns and thistles are to spring up; fourthly, upon the man who, after a struggle with unfriendly nature, will return once more to the dust of the ground from which he was taken. A noticeable feature of this oracle is the interconnexion between its parts. It all hangs together. For example, as the destiny of the woman and the fate of the serpent meet in the promise to the woman's seed, so also the toil of Adam is interwoven with the curse upon the ground, from which he originated,[3] while to the sorrows of the woman are added the overlordship of the man.

Now in the corresponding section of Romans 8 the tragedy of

---

[1] For 're-birth' in scripture in its relation to the teaching of St Paul see *Dominion*, Ch. V, §§ iv and v. When due regard is given to the whole sequence of images drawn from natural processes re-birth may be seen to be implicit in 2 Cor. 5^{17} and in Rom. 6^5.

[2] Rom. 8^{19-23}.

[3] As from it is derived his very name—*Adham* from *adhamah*.

creation as a whole, as subjected to 'vanity' by the fall, has in
like manner been assimilated to the sorrowful child-bearing of
the woman. This interpretation is true to the spirit of the story.
For in the biblical conception Eve, 'the mother of all living',
was created to fulfil a function which in a wider sense was shared
by all the creatures—the function, that is, of co-operating with
Adam in his dominion. In this she was the representative of all
creation. In the fourfold curse Adam sinks back into identity
with the earth from which he took his origin. So also, in the
apostolic interpretation, the share of all creation in the consequences of the fall is typified by a corresponding identification
of mother earth with the sorrowful travail of mother Eve.[1]
Mother Eve brought forth Cain, the murderer. But a new Eve
brought forth the new Adam, the victorious seed, to whose
image 'the rest of her seed' shall be conformed in the day of
resurrection.[2] Mother earth brings forth thorns and thistles. But
when that day dawns for which the whole creation groans and
travails there is the promise of release from such blight and
blemish in a yet wider transformation. As the frustrated parturi-
tion of the earth was redeemed by the child-bearing of the new
Eve, so too the corruption and degradation which fallen man
has brought upon his world will pass away. Whereas through
his fall Adam descended into the dust of the earth, hereafter, in
the re-birth of all things, the treasures of earth will be taken up
into that bodily life which is conformed to the image of God's
Son. Thus all creation will partake in 'the liberty of the glory
of the children of God'.[3]

vi

Connexions between the theologies of St Paul and of the
Revelation. They both use the Jewish symbolism of heavenly

[1] For the idea cp. 2 Esdras 10[1-15]. See also *Dominion*, pp. 40, 148 *f*, with notes.

[2] Rom. 8[29], where the Pauline phrase: 'that he might be the first-born
among many brethren' corresponds exactly to the expression cited in the
text from Rev. 12[17].

[3] The twice repeated στενάζομεν in 2 Cor. 5[2-4] is connected with the
desire for 'nakedness' to be clothed (cp. Gen. 2[25], 3[7-11, 21]), whereas here
this word is connected with 'travail' in childbirth. These facts suggest that
Gen. 3 is also part of the background in 2 Cor. 5 as it is in Rom. 8. Cp. above,
the second note to the second par. of this section.

garments, but with a difference. This follows from (*a*) the fact that Christ's body was raised from the tomb and (*b*) the present share of Christians in his risen life. In Revelation the symbolism includes both Pauline aspects (continuity and discontinuity): (1) heavenly garments cover the nakedness of sinners; but (2) earthly garments, when washed 'in the blood of the Lamb', become heavenly.

St Paul's picture of creation in travail recalls St John's vision of the new Eve travailing in the midst of creation (Revelation 12[1]). We are also reminded of a like affinity between the vision of the New Jerusalem and the Pauline statement about the heavenly citizenship of the church in Philippi.[1] This passage (Philippians 3[17-21]) begins with a contrast between the earthly and the heavenly; and, like 1 Corinthians 15, it connects the resurrection of man with Christ's restoration of Adam's dominion.[2] For the restored dominion will be finally manifested in that crowning event. Here the low estate of the visible church is signified by our lowly body, which through sharing the humiliation of Jesus is being united with the scars in *his* flesh, that in *our* mortal flesh 'the life also of Jesus may be manifested'.[3] 'But if we have become united with the likeness of his death' through being grafted into him in baptism 'then we shall also be united with the likeness of his resurrection'.[4] These earlier statements of the apostle explain the confidence with which, despite his earthly sojourn in a distant frontier-post of the heavenly Zion, he yet awaits the final epiphany of 'our Saviour, the Lord Jesus Christ, who shall fashion anew the body of our humiliation that it may be conformed to the body of his glory, according to the working whereby he is able to subdue all things unto himself'.[5]

The connexion between the theologies of St Paul and St John the divine can be clearly seen in yet another section of the Revelation, in which there appears 'a great multitude . . . standing before the throne and before the Lamb, clothed in white robes with palms in their hands' (7[9-17]). The white robes here represent the risen bodies of the saints. This mode of speech is, as we have seen, sometimes used by St Paul; and when this

---

[1] See above, Ch. II, § iv.
[2] cp. 1 Cor. 15[26, 27] with Phil. 3[21]. The reference in both is to Ps. 8[6].
[3] 2 Cor. 4[10, 11]; cp. Phil. 2[8].
[4] Rom. 6[5].   [5] Phil. 3[21].

happens the resurrection body is thought of as a heavenly garment which may be put on over the earthly garment of mortal flesh. Jewish writers also used this 'clothing' symbolism at that period. There is, however, a significant difference. Whereas it was a characteristic Jewish belief that the mortal body would be put off and replaced by a heavenly 'garment', yet there appears to be nothing comparable to the Pauline belief in a hidden process going on in the earthly 'tent-house' which was vitally connected with the building of the risen body. The Jewish notion might be said to correspond more closely to the idea contained in Zechariah 3^{3-5} where the high-priest receives rich apparel in exchange for filthy garments. Even in *The Ascension of Isaiah*, in spite of Christian editing, the typically Jewish conception is retained.

It will be recalled, however, that St Paul sometimes employed quite different language, as in Romans 8^{11} and Philippians 3^{21}. In these later epistles he recurs to the thought that in some sense our present mortal body will be changed into the glorious body. Moreover, we are left in no doubt as to the source of this language, so new and revolutionary as it was from a purely Jewish point of view. For in his earliest statement upon the subject the apostle explains that this is precisely what happened when Christ rose from the dead.[1] The mortal body which was laid in the tomb was transformed into the risen body. So two facts separated the Christian belief from the purely Jewish way of thinking, namely, first the resurrection of our Lord from the tomb, and secondly our present share in his risen life; the second fact is inseparably bound up with the first through our having been mystically united with Jesus in his death and resurrection by our baptism. At this point we can resume our comparison of the Pauline teaching with that form of the clothing symbolism which is to be found in the Revelation. In that book the writer frequently refers to the resurrection body in the Jewish language of heavenly garments. But, as we shall see, he does so in a distinctively Christian way. Moreover, under this single mode of speech he combines the complementary truths which we have found to be characteristic of St Paul.

The references to this subject in the Revelation are dominated by two leading ideas, namely, first man's need for gar-

[1] I Cor. 15^{1-20}, on which see *The Common Life*, Ch. IX, pp. 257*ff*.

ments to cover his nakedness, and secondly the necessity that his garments should be cleansed and preserved from defilement. The former idea goes back to the story of Adam and Eve whose disobedience caused them to be ashamed of their nakedness.[1] This feature of the story constitutes a profound allegory of sin's nature and effects. In St Paul's phrase sinners fall short of the divine glory.[2] It no longer covers them; for they have departed from it. Yet they need that glory desperately; and when conscience is active they become aware of their uncovered state— the nakedness of a false independence which cannot abide the consuming glance of God.[3] Incidentally, this is a good example of the way in which a given piece of biblical symbolism in its fuller development transcends the conscious thought of its human originators. The conclusion of the story carries a further suggestion.[4] The coats of skin with which Adam and Eve were clothed by God point forward to a divine provision by which the sinner's nakedness may be covered, thus foreshadowing the heavenly garments of the resurrection.

We pass now to the second leading idea in the Revelation. The garments offered or promised to sinners and worn by the saints are constantly referred to as *white* garments.[5] Moreover, in the vision of the great multitude 'clothed in white robes' a new and significant detail appears. The seer is told that these holy ones 'washed their robes and made them white in the blood of the Lamb' (7^{14}). In other words the earthly garments which they already possessed were, by this mystical washing, transformed into heavenly garments. A further detail is added in the final beatitude of the book (22^{14}), where we are told that 'they who wash their robes' have right of access to 'the tree of life' and may 'enter by the gates into the city', that is the heavenly Jerusalem. The exquisite subtlety, and yet beautiful simplicity, of this phraseology are bound up with its Hebrew idioms of thought. Behind such words lie, on the one hand, a wide and varied use of 'clothing' symbolism in the Old Testament, and on the other hand the Hebrew habit of treating soul and body

[1] Gen. 2^{25}, 3^{7-11}.   [2] Rom. 3^{23}.

[3] The Laodicean church, sunk in complacency, was unaware of its nakedness (Rev. 3^{18}).

[4] For which see *Dominion*, pp. 93 f and notes.

[5] Rev. $3^{5, 18}$, 4^4, 6^{11}, $7^{9, 13}$, 19^{14}.

as a single animated being without distinction, or, again, of identifying 'soul' qualities with 'body' forms. Thus in Psalm 104[1, 2] two consecutive sentences tell us that God is 'clothed with honour and majesty' and that he covers himself 'with light as with a garment'. Here the Hebrew mind first thinks of inward qualities as outward clothing and then quickly carries the imagery on into the phenomena of creation. Thus qualities are projected into material forms.[1] It is already clear that this way of thinking will throw fresh light on the puzzling Pauline dichotomy.[2]

<h1 style="text-align:center">vii</h1>

Christ, our body-garment of righteousness, is also embodied in his members. As on the transfigured Christ, the 'whitened' garments of the baptized anticipate the risen body. The highpriestly robe of God the Word first covered his creation, and then recovered it in the lowly form of the Servant, the sacrificial garment with which Christians are clothed. The risen life belongs to a transformed creation in which death has become a function of deathless life. This secret of creation, laid open in a mystery of dying and rising, the world cannot recognize; yet the 'otherness' of its distinctive form cannot be surrendered.

In Revelation 7[14] and elsewhere in that book there is a double significance in the heavenly garments which may be illustrated from two sayings in the book of Job. In the first of these Job says to God: 'Thou hast clothed me with skin and flesh.'[3] There we have the notion of the body-garment. In the second passage Job says: 'I put on righteousness, and it clothed itself with me.'[4] In this case the relationship is mutual. Righteousness is the man's garment; but also the man becomes the body-garment of his righteousness. We are reminded here of two Pauline sayings: 'Ye are in Christ Jesus who became to us from God . . . righteousness' and 'As many of you as were baptized into Christ did put on Christ' (as a garment).[5] The One Man Jesus Christ be-

---

[1] Another example, occurring in Rom. 7[23], was cited in Ch. 3, § vii. There what we should call psychological factors are regarded as 'members' of the body.

[2] See above, end of § iv.   [3] Job 10[11]; cp. Ezek. 37[6, 8].

[4] Job 29[14] (RV margin, supported by Driver and Gray in ICC).

[5] 1 Cor. 1[30], Gal. 3[27]; cp. Isa. 11[5], 52[1], 61[10], Jer. 23[6], 33[16].

came the body-garment of righteousness with which, in baptism, we were clothed. Yet, with equal truth we may say that he, as our righteousness, is embodied corporately in us, since we are his mystical body, and again, that he is embodied corporeally in our bodies, since they are his members.[1] On the other hand the body-garment which we inherit from Adam is, in St Paul's phrase, 'the body of sin'.[2] Clothed therein we confess that 'all our righteousnesses are as a polluted garment'.[3] This defilement, however, we washed away in baptism when we 'whitened' our garments in the blood of the Lamb,[4] and thereby entered into his righteousness.[5]

The language of the Revelation is here reminiscent of the transfiguration story as told by St Mark. For in that scene our Lord's garments became 'white, as no fuller on earth can *whiten* them', where the same word is used as in Revelation 7[14].[6] Again, according to the other accounts the dazzling whiteness of the Lord's garments was 'like the light'.[7] Jesus was clothed in that uncreated light of glory which is lacking to Adam's fallen race. The risen bodies of the saints, however, will shine with that same splendour of divine glory which Jesus wore as a garment upon the mount.[8] The mystery of the transfiguration which is enacted in the church and in the sacraments will receive its ultimate fulfilment in the resurrection of man. In this respect, however, the harvest is already like the firstfruits. The integral character of the new creation is manifested in the life of the church, as in the gospel story. The traditional white robe which the neophyte put on at his baptism signified that the old self had become a new creature. But it also signified that the end is implicit in the beginning. As the transfiguration of Jesus foreshadowed his resurrection, so the same mystery of transfiguration re-enacted in the church foreshadows the resurrection of

---

[1] 1 Cor. 6[15].   [2] Rom. 6[6].   [3] Isa. 64[6];cp. Jude[23].

[4] The active verb in Rev. 7[14] corresponds to the phrase: 'ye washed yourselves' in 1 Cor. 6[11].

[5] In 1 John 1[5]–2[2] those who are cleansed in the blood of the Righteous One walk in the light; with which cp. what follows in the text.

[6] Mark 9[3].

[7] Matt. 17[2]; cp. Luke 9[29]. In the four gospels white garments are connected with the Easter story.

[8] cp. Dan. 12[3], to which corresponds 1 Cor. 15[40–44] by contrast with Rom. 3[23].

man. In both of these foreshadowings, however, time is transcended; for the reality foreshadowed is not simply a future event.

In the gospel story the glory is already present in the humiliation; and so it is also in the church. We who were transformed by the cleansing blood of the Lamb in the waters of baptism are already clothed in that garment of divine glory which will hereafter be manifestly ours. For when we died with Christ we began to live his risen life, since death and resurrection form one mystery in the new creation. Elsewhere in the Revelation the Lamb, in whose blood the saints 'washed their robes and whitened them', is identified with 'the Word of God' who is also 'the Alpha and the Omega, the first and the last, the beginning and the end'.[1] The predestined victim, whose transfigured form was seen upon the mount, is the source and site of creation. Moreover, the bright garment which covered him is the garment of righteousness, that sacrificial love which is the very texture of divine glory.[2] It is the high-priestly robe of God the Word, with which, in the beginning, he clothed his creation.[3] When man was crowned with glory and honour that he might exercise priestly dominion, this was his covering.

The covering, however, was lost. We might say that it slipped from the shoulders of the first Adam when his own act of disobedience stripped him naked. So the Word himself put on the lowly form of the Servant, and in so doing clothed himself afresh with his sacerdotal garment of righteousness and sprinkled it with the blood of his own sacrifice. By this act of obedience he provided fine linen to adorn his bride. Her marriage garment, however, is woven out of many strands. For it consists in the new righteousness of all the saints.[4] Sprinkled with the blood of the Lamb, their garments also have become the pure vesture of the sanctuary. The 'great multitude which no man could number' are thus a priestly company, a worshipping community. 'Therefore are they before the throne of God' and offer to him unceasing worship in his temple.[5] The scene is in the New Jerusalem, where, in fulfilment of prophecy,[6] God 'shall spread

---

[1] Rev. 19[13], 22[13]. Significantly both titles occur in close connexion with heavenly garments. Cp. 19[8, 13, 14] and 22[14].

[2] cp. the OT refs. in the third note of this section.

[3] See above, §i, par. 2.   [4] Rev. 19[7-14].

[5] Rev. 7[14, 15].   [6] Isa. 4[5, 6], Ezek. 37[21-28].

his tabernacle over them'. Now, when 'the cloud covered the tent of meeting' in the wilderness, 'the glory of the Lord filled' it and made it his dwelling-place (Exodus 40³⁴). Thus in the saints, as in the Christ, the earthen vessel of the flesh was from the first lit up with the sacrificial flame of his obedience. This condition they entered into in their baptism, when they too received the form of the Servant. The hidden process which followed corresponded to the hidden glory of the transfiguration, containing within it in germinal form the whole mystery of the final transformation through death and resurrection.

The vision of the great multitude concludes in a typical scene of prophecy fulfilled which shows the risen glory of the saints in a setting of creation transformed;[1] just as in Romans 8 St Paul connects the resurrection of man with the re-birth of the world. For in Christ there is renovation and fulfilment, not only of sanctified persons, but also of the whole creation; and this transformation takes place within a new world-order whose outward form is vitally significant since it manifests the new organism of the Christ. To that outward order belong the risen bodies of the saints; and to its single pattern the mystery of resurrection in all its aspects corresponds. So, for example, the apostolic writers do not evade the grim facts of physical death and of bodily dissolution. They do not ignore the gulf which separates the flesh and blood of our present physical frame from the future body of glory. They show, however, that this deep disjunction is, for those who are in Christ, included within a much vaster mystery. Jesus conquered death by taking it into his own life, by making it (so to speak) a function of that life which is itself deathless. Moreover, those who 'put on Christ' and 'keep their garments'[2] are already being conformed in their whole being to that organism whose sacrificial character makes dying to be an integral factor in life itself.

For such, therefore, the decay of this present physical frame in death is not radically different from that which is already taking place in our mortal flesh. It is not altogether unlike the peeling off of the outer crust from a wounded member of the body after the wound has healed. The destruction[3] of that

---

[1] Rev. 7¹⁶, ¹⁷ and Isa. 49¹⁰.   [2] Rev. 16¹⁵.

[3] 'Detachment' would perhaps represent more accurately what happens to matter no longer organic to life.

which is no longer integral to the life of the organism is a condition by which the organism as a whole is set free to enter into a new and more fitting form. This far-reaching law of creation is implicit in St Paul's use of analogy. In a fallen world its full significance has been obscured; but in the sacrifice of Christ the mystery of creation, in this as in other respects, has been laid open.[1] Through death and resurrection this law of creation comes to its highest fulfilment in that 'temple of the body' to which we belong. The ending of St Mark's Gospel (16^{12}) tells us that the risen Lord was manifested to two disciples in 'another form'. So, too, in the visible church the 'otherness' of the risen form is foreshadowed and to some extent anticipated. Moreover, the sacrificial life which integrates dying and rising in one mystery is something 'other' than the earthly way of life which the world can recognize. It is in itself inscrutable, being laid open only to faith. For it partakes in the 'other form' under the veil of our present humiliation. Nevertheless, this hidden life of the church is integral salvation in process of restoring creation. Consequently some at least of its fruits are evident. But those which the world *can* appreciate are not the most important, being by-products of a life not directly orientated towards them, as the humanism of a St Francis springs from his absorption in the love of God.

The otherness of the new creation inevitably sets it in tension with the life of a fallen world; and this fact is indeed a source of danger, but also of strength. The 'other form' within which the splendour of the resurrection is being prepared is veiled under the low estate of the visible church. In its present outer garb it is the lowly form of the Servant; and this very outwardness of the visible church can, therefore, be an occasion of scandal. Thus, the external fixity of creed, ministry and sacraments may seem to be a veil of the flesh which hides the glory, as surely as it also foreshadows the rich concreteness of a bodily resurrection. So a wave of false spirituality may tempt the church to surrender her own God-given outward form, or some part of it, in the vain hope of more easily providing a soul for the secular order of the world. The hope is vain; because the hidden life of dying and rising with Christ cannot be preserved in a state of nakedness. The new righteousness which constitutes an eternal

---

[1] See again, Ch. IV, last par. but two, and Ch. V, § i, par. 2.

challenge to human pride and selfishness must be clothed in its
own proper body-garment, if it is so to leaven the all-flesh of
mankind as to transform it. A righteousness which is not so
embodied will soon be secularized, exchanging the form of the
Servant for the gaudy, yet essentially shoddy, garments of cheap
utopian fashion. The 'body of sin' cannot be whitened by any
earthly fuller. It must be washed in the blood of the Lamb.

viii

The intermediate state. Phil. 1$^{21, 23}$ indicates a fuller form of
life in Christ between death and resurrection. Probation and conflict succeeded by rest and fruition. Continuity 'in Christ' at a
higher level. Finality of 'justification' attained in death through
release from 'the body of sin' (Rom. 6$^{6, 7}$). Implications of the
'clothing' symbolism. Its two aspects in Rev. 7^{14} and 6^{11} correspond to the duality of Pauline thought concerning the transition
through death. So in Rev. 20$^{4-6}$ we see the triumph of 'the whole
Christ' in the present dispensation.

Up to this point we have been considering the resurrection of
the body primarily in its relation to our present earthly existence.
The bridging of that gulf, however, inevitably involves us in a
further problem. How are we to regard the intermediate state
into which the Christian enters after death? We have already
arrived at solid ground for the conviction that there is a continuity of the risen life which is unbroken by death. How far
then does scripture lift the veil still further to indicate the nature
of that existence which is the prelude to general resurrection
and final judgement? We shall find definite information upon
this subject, as before, both in St Paul's epistles and in the
Revelation of St John; and it will be convenient to consider the
evidence in that order. We will begin by citing an important
statement from the Epistle to the Philippians, to which reference has already been made:[1]

To me to live is Christ, and to die is gain . . . having the desire to
depart and be with Christ; for it is very far better (Philippians i.
21, 23).

This pronouncement takes us a good deal further than the

[1] See above, § iv, last three pars.

earlier statement in 2 Corinthians 5$^{2-10}$, although there also the apostle would be 'well-pleased rather to be absent from the body and to be present with the Lord'; and this implies a nearer intimacy with his Saviour in the latter state. Moreover there, as here, he submits himself to the Lord's will. In the later passage, however, his tone is much more positive. Indeed, this utterance stands out as a classic statement of faith with regard to the Christian attitude towards death. It consists of two sentences, in each of which death seems to be regarded as the gateway into a fuller form of the life in Christ. If 'to live is Christ, and to die is gain', then it would follow that all the rich significance of the Christian life, as elsewhere described by the apostle, is carried forward to a higher stage after death. This estimate is corroborated by the second sentence. For, although 'to live is Christ', yet 'to depart' means to 'be with Christ' in a sense which 'is very far better'. Moreover, it is clear that the apostle is not here thinking of a distant heavenly bliss beyond the intermediate state. He is speaking of a condition which follows immediately upon death.

It does not follow, however, that this statement excludes the notion of an intermediate state. For in an earlier epistle he makes it clear that our filial relation to God in Christ is to be fully attained only in 'the redemption of our body' (Romans 8^{23}). Also in 1 Corinthians 15 he affirms that the prophetic saying: 'Death is swallowed up in victory' will be fulfilled only in that great transformation when 'the dead shall be raised incorruptible' (verses 51–54). It would appear, then, that death is not the end of our pilgrimage, but rather the gateway into a more advanced stage of that pilgrimage wherein some grave hindrances which at present hamper us have been removed. As to the details scripture maintains a wholesome reserve. Yet important conclusions may be drawn from what is said. For example, whereas after death the soul is disembodied, at the final judgement 'we have all to appear before the tribunal of Christ, each to be requited for what he has done with his body, well or ill'.[1] From this it follows that the period of probation ends with death. The conflict with temptation is now a thing of the past; yet its consequences continue. Both truths recur in Revelation 14^{13}, where we read:

[1] 2 Cor. 5^{10} (M).

Blessed are the dead who die in the Lord from henceforth; yea saith the Spirit, that they may rest from their labours; for their works do follow with them.

The blessedness of the holy souls is here shewn to have two aspects. They are no longer labouring; they rest from toil. Yet on the other hand this state of rest is not negative. For it is a condition into which the fruits of past labours enter. All that is positive and significant in the earthly life is somehow carried over into this second stage of our pilgrimage, where fruitful activity is the counterpart of restful refreshment. Moreover, the close association of 'rest' with 'works', in the words of the 'voice from heaven' just now quoted, corresponds markedly with our Lord's own words concerning the Creator's eternal sabbath rest in the other great Johannine book:[1] 'My Father worketh hitherto, and I work.' Such an analogy with the divine life recalls to mind the text from Philippians, where emphasis falls upon the fact that the life beyond death is 'very far better' precisely because it is a being 'with Christ'. If it be supposed that we cannot generalize from the case of one so pre-eminent as St Paul, it may be pointed out that in scripture the apostle is reported to have described himself as 'the chief of sinners' and therefore also as a typical instance of the divine mercy to all believers.[2] If then we may regard his statement as typical there is one further conclusion to be drawn from it. If it places the departed souls in a position of advantage over those Christians who are still living the earthly life, it also, and with equal emphasis, indicates a continuity of pattern, in that both stages of the Christian pilgrimage are centred in Christ. The connexion between these two facts must next be considered.

The faithful departed are members of Christ; and so, although 'absent from the body', they are 'present with the Lord' *in his Body*. However changed their situation may be, their life is still one of identification with their Saviour in his sacrificial humanity. In the eucharistic memorial of his sacrifice we appropriately remember them in our prayers precisely because they are redeemed sinners in whom the effects of that sacrifice are still operative. Yet, notwithstanding the continuity, death has made a difference. So now we turn to another aspect of the apostle's

---

[1] John 5[17].
[2] I Tim. I[15, 16].

teaching where, in Romans 6, he describes the saving significance of baptism:

> Our old man was crucified with Christ, that the body of sin might
> be done away, that so we should no longer be in bondage to sin; for
> he that is dead has been justified from sin (Romans 6[6, 7]).

In baptism we were identified with our Lord in his death on the
cross. Now in scripture death is the penalty for sin; and our
Lord in his death bore the penalty for our sins, thereby securing
for us escape from the bondage of sin in all its forms. In baptism,
we died to sin 'that the body of sin might be done away'; and by
union with Christ we have no part in sin. Yet this fleshly body
of ours is still a vehicle of the old fallen nature. So long as we are
in the body, therefore, we are subject to the assaults of evil. We
still harbour what St Paul calls 'the mind of the flesh', so that
our nature, being divided, is the scene of unceasing conflict.
This state of things is brought to an end by physical death. So
the justification effected when we died with Christ in baptism
becomes permanent for the faithful Christian when the soul is
released from the body. Then at last the words become wholly
and finally true: 'He that is dead has been justified from sin.'

So he continues: 'If we died with Christ, we believe that we
shall also live with him.' This saying also has its partial fulfilment now, since 'our life is hid with Christ in God' (Colossians
3[3]). Yet Jesus 'died unto sin once for all' (Romans 6[10]) in the
most literal and physical sense; and there will come a time when
this will happen to us too, as it has already happened to a great
multitude of departed Christians. Thus far we may draw a
parallel between the saving death of Jesus and every holy Christian death. In such a parallel, however, there is not only likeness but also inevitable contrast. Our Saviour's pilgrimage
ended with the death which constituted final victory; ours continues through a period of waiting. Yet, although they still wait
for heavenly bliss, the departed souls have been released from
'the body of sin', and therefore they may, and surely do, anticipate in some considerable degree the consummation of their
hope in Christ. This conclusion seems to follow inevitably from
much of the apostolic teaching already considered, and not least
from the implications of continuity contained in the picture of
garments washed white in the blood of the Lamb. Here, how-

ever, we must remember that in the biblical image-thinking no single image can possibly convey all aspects of the truth. There is in fact another application of the clothing symbolism to which we must now give our attention.

The imagery of Revelation 7[14], taken by itself, might seem to suggest that the vital transformation of the saints took place when they became Christians, and that all that followed was inevitable consequence. It might even be supposed to mean that 'the resurrection had passed already' in a sense which would render a final transformation unnecessary.[1] Fortunately, however, the author has another picture which presents another facet of the mystery. In Chapter 6 (verses 9–11) we read that he 'saw under the altar' the souls of the Christian martyrs and heard them crying for vengeance upon their murderers, whereupon 'there was given to each one of them a white garment', and they were bidden 'to rest yet a little while until' the martyred host was completed. Upon this we have here only one comment to make.[2] In Hebrew idiom the souls of the martyrs are identified with their spilt blood which automatically makes its claim upon divine justice, because the souls have been rendered naked, and in a certain sense homeless, through being violently deprived of their body-garments.[3] If they are to be at rest they must be clothed once more. So each receives a white garment and with it an invitation to rest. So they 'rest from their labours' as in 14[13]; and this restful waiting is, through the symbolism of the white garment, marked out as a stage further along the path towards the final transformation into the fulness of the risen life.

The contrast between these two pictures (Revelation 6[11] and 7[14]) suggests that there can be considerable elasticity in the use of such symbolism. Moreover, there is a parallel with Pauline oscillation between continuity and discontinuity which underlines the apostolic thesis that in the Christian way of living death is simply a function of life. Of this one further illustration may be given from Revelation 20[4–6], the passage which depicts a millennial reign of the Christ and his saints after a 'first resurrec-

---

[1] This is presumably the heresy referred to in 2 Tim. 2[18].

[2] For fuller details upon this and what follows see *Additional Note B* below.

[3] cp. 2 Cor. 5[1 *ff*].

tion'. Here traditional Jewish material is used in a way which can have an entirely new Christian meaning. As St Augustine saw, there is nothing here which can be fairly held to support an earthly millennium in the sense of popular Jewish and some patristic expectation. The 'first resurrection' may be baptismal, or it may refer to the privileged condition of the martyred saints in the total economy of the Christian dispensation, their peculiar share in the risen glory of the Christ and their partnership with him in the restored dominion. Here the Pauline contrast between 'earthly' and 'heavenly' has disappeared. For in the present reign of the ascended Christ heaven and earth and all that lies between are united in one transcendent mystery.

Additional Note B.

The symbolism of the Johannine Revelation

In the preceding chapter (§ ii, second paragraph) it was remarked that the author of the Revelation has two ways of speaking in reference to the resurrection of the dead. The 'two ways' are (1) 'white garments' and (2) 'the first resurrection' with its sequel in 20[4-6]. These are referred to successively in the final paragraph preceding this note;[1] and, despite obvious differences, a certain parallel can be there observed. For both forms of speech depict a symbolic prelude to the general resurrection, one in which the final transformation is in some sense anticipated. There is, moreover, a further point of agreement between 6[11] and 20[4-6]. Both the white robes and 'the first resurrection' are privileges granted to the faithful *after* death, although nothing is said which could rule out the Pauline doctrine of a risen life *before* death. Presumably the author saw no inconsistency between the two contrasted pictures in 6[11] and 7[14]; and if we examine an earlier passage fresh light upon this will appear. White garments are first mentioned by this author in 3[4, 5]. In those verses it is said that among Christians living in Sardis there were a few who 'did not defile their garments'. Here is a counterpart to the imagery in 7[14]. The suggestion would seem to be that these Christians had preserved their baptismal innocence.

There follows a statement to the effect that they will 'walk in white' with the risen Christ; and as the statement proceeds it certainly looks beyond death ('he that overcometh') even to the final

---

[1] For 20[4-6] see the judicious statement of H. B. Swete in his commentary *ad loc.* (pp. 260*ff*).

judgement, when the victor's name will be found in 'the book of life' to be confessed 'before my Father and before his angels'. Moreover, after the individual victory has been won it is once more affirmed that the victor will be clothed in white garments. This statement is so worded that it might be understood to mean simply a continuity of the risen life through the crisis of death or actual renewal of the heavenly garments after death. By contrast, a few verses later (3^{18}) we learn that Christians living in Laodicea need to be spiritually re-clothed. The statement in $3^{4, 5}$ is so comprehensive that, by implication, it appears to include within itself everything that this author has to say about the risen life of the saints. On the other hand the scattered references in Jewish apocalyptic shew nothing comparable concerning continuity through death and transformation. A possible exception to this statement might be cited from *The Apocalypse of Baruch* (Chs. 49–52), where a preliminary resuscitation of the mortal body is made before the judgement and, again, a final transformation into glory after the judgement. The latter, indeed, recalls the Pauline language of Phil. 3^{21}. There is, however, no inherent or necessary continuity between these two resurrections. The first is made solely for the sake of mutual recognition. It has a characteristic Hebrew emphasis upon the necessary unity of soul and body in a complete personality. Thus it is effected for a purely practical purpose which in no way foreshadows the final transformation.

INDEX

The numbering of biblical chapters and verses follows RV, except where, in (i) (a) a different numeration is indicated for the Hebrew text (H) or the Septuagint (LXX). For this see p. 71nn. The letters 'n' or 'nn' indicate the footnotes of this volume.

(i) REFERENCES

(ii) PERSONS

(iii) SUBJECTS